At this holiday season, the most precious gifts
we can offer are things mere money can't buy: time…thought…creativity
…a singular gift made with our own hands.
Each of us has such a priceless memory tucked away somewhere in a secret
place, a reminder of a special Christmas morning when we untied a package
to discover a one-of-a-kind treasure made especially for us.
Hand-stitched linens, embroidered decorations and holiday finery
of a gentler era, fashioned by our mothers,
grandmothers and aunts, fill our holiday dreams.
As we become the keepers of Christmas, we share a bit of ourselves.
Wrap a memory in tissue and ribbon…a gift made by caring hands
filled with love.

───────────── ❧ ─────────────

Printed in the United States of America.
ISBN: 0-9660674-0-1
First Printing: 1997

Editor: Ann M. Henderson
Assistant Editor: Dianne B. Boney
Design: Cassandra Dowling
Cover Photography: Charles Turner

Project Designers: Kathy Albright, Paris Bottman, Hope Carr, Roberta Chase, Carol Clements, Janelle Cox, Lucy Crosby, Jennifer Crutcher, Cassandra Dowling, April Dunn, Pat Ferebee, Geri Frazier, Connie Harbor, Janet Hierl, Trudy Horne, Lou Anne Lamar, Tina Lewis, Neal McQuinn, Barbara Meger, Bev Moore, Delbra W. Moore, Nancy Newell, T. Lu Nixon, Martha Parker, Susan Porter, Jody B. Raines, Esther Randall, Rosemary Sandberg-Padden, Suzanne Sawko, Sharon Sparks, Pam Sprinkle, Mollie Jane Taylor, Chris DeMars Victorsen, Carolyn Walker, Chery Williams

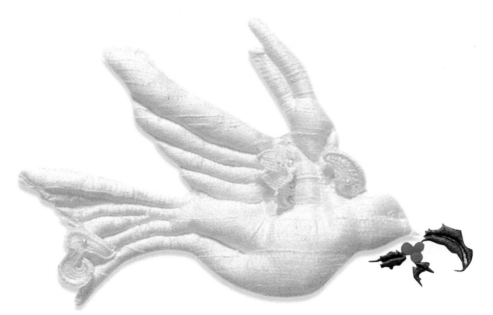

A CREATIVE NEEDLE
Christmas

Needle Publishing Inc., Lookout Mountain, Georgia, U S A

My special thanks to Cassandra Dowling whose vision and sense of design ensured a beautiful book; Trudy Horne and Jennelle Robertson for precision and grace in stitching the cover, Janice Ferguson for providing them just the right pieces of lace; Tina Lewis for bringing a festive spirit of enthusiasm to every project she encounters, no matter what the season; Pam Newberry for boundless energy and organization; Charlie Stevens for helpful advice beyond the call of duty; Dianne Boney for commitment and attention to detail on countless late nights and weekends; the host of talented designers with whom I've had the pleasure of working over the last decade; and my daughter, Halle for nourishment of body and soul.

————— ❦ —————

SET A BEAUTIFUL TABLE

Enhance your
holiday repast with
delicate linens,
embroidered napkins,
traditional
Christmas crackers,
and ribbon-edged
table runner.
"Perfect
Poinsettias" napkin
and placemat
instructions on
page 92.

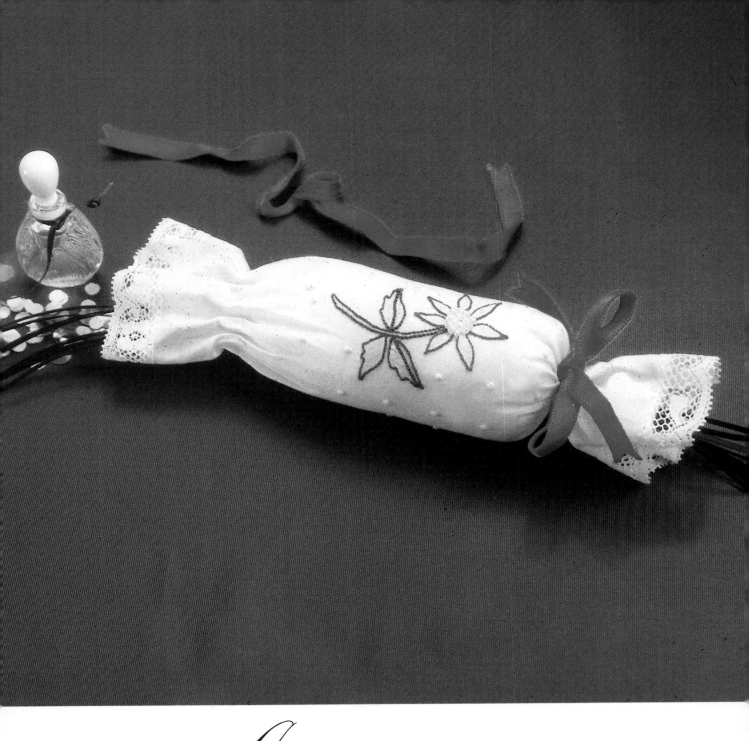

*A*n exquisite placemat, napkin and bread server in Battenburg lace and linen add a touch of elegance to any holiday meal. "Battenburg Linens for the Holidays" instructions on page 89. ⚘ An embroidered Christmas cracker can be refilled year after year with trinkets and treasures. Just pull a ribbon and see what surprises spill out! "Christmas Crackers" instructions on page 90. ⚘

*M*oiré and tapestry ribbon dress
your table in holiday finery. Complete the look with
matching napkin rings. "Festive Table Setting" instructions
on page 95. ❧   Linen squares with scalloped edges and
poinsettia appliqués are stitched entirely by machine. "Perfect
Poinsettias" instructions on page 92. ❧

A *satin-stitched candy cane and dotted ribbon streamers create a festive Christmas Cracker. Design and "Christmas Cracker" instructions on page 90.* ❧ *Ordinary napkins become extraordinary with a quick touch of machine embroidery and a gold cord bow. "Christmas Tree Napkin" instructions on page 96.* ❧

CHRISTMAS TREE ORNAMENTS

Fragrant pine boughs, glimmering lights and shiny globes of glass bring this magical season to life. Add your own special touches of treasured lace, silky ribbon and delicate embroidery to create traditions your family will remember for all the holidays to come.

*D̶ainty embroidered panels are joined
with lace beading. Add hangers of ribbon rosettes, and tuck
these heirloom treasures into the branches of the family tree.
"Christmas Collectibles" embroidery design and instructions
on page 98. ❧ Chubby cherubs flutter their lacy wings through
tree branches. "Christmas Cherubs" instructions on
page 100. ❧*

*E*ntwined with golden cords, ribbons and silk roses, lush Victorian cones suspend tiny treasures on your holiday tree. *"Victorian Cornucopias"* instructions on page 103. ❧ A sky of midnight blue glitters with stars and a golden half-moon which offers a comfy seat for Santa during his travels. *"Santa-in-the-Moon"* graph and instructions on page 104. ❧

*A*ntricate Battenburg lace is shaped into delicate trims to bedeck special packages or tree branches. "A Battenburg Christmas" instructions on page 106.

ecorate a holiday wreath or an entire tree with these Battenburg ornaments which represent Christian symbols of faith. A single ornament attached to a satin ribbon makes a lovely bookmark—and a perfect little gift. "Christian Symbols in Battenburg" instructions on page 108.

ilvery spider webs are the decorative finish and focal point for shimmering smocked ornaments. "Sparkling Smocked Ornament" instructions on page 112. ❧ Capture Christmas memories for years to come with a moiré and Swiss batiste frame ornament. Shadow embroidery and granito snowflakes are surrounded with a golden cord and tassels. "Picture Ornament" instructions on page 115. ❧

ALL THROUGH T

HE HOUSE

*Thoughts of
home capture our
hearts
at Christmastime.
Whether we're
decking the halls,
trimming the tree,
or sipping egg nog
by the fireside,
the holiday mood
pervades every
room.*

atchwork fragments of velvets, cotton
tartans and calicos are dotted with silk ribbon embroidery
and lace motifs. Stitch individual squares into a duvet cover,
or a holiday stocking. "Crazy Patch Duvet Cover"
instructions on page 117. ❧

*S*umptuous Ultrasuede® is trimmed with gold in this exceptional tree skirt. Graceful swans glide around its creamy border. This is a project to display proudly for years. "Swan Tree Skirt" instructions on page 118. ❧ Red moiré is adorned with Battenburg lace for an elegant look no Santa could resist. "Battenburg Stocking" instructions on page 120. ❧

*W*ings of embroidery edged in pearls, satin ribbon tied into a bow, silk holly leaves and delicate twigs give distinct personalities to a heavenly band of angels. Stitch them all from one basic pattern. Add a halo and a ribbon wreath, and stitch one for every room in the house. "Heavenly Host of Angels" instructions on page 122. ❧

mbroidered bunnies frolic in the snow on a cuffed linen stocking, edged with green wool piping and tiny silver jingle bells. "Snowbunnies" instructions on page 123. ❧ Scraps of fabric and fragments of lace are stitched in a Victorian patchwork design. Edges are outlined with pearls and topped with ribbon streamers. "Victorian Christmas Stocking" instructions on page 124. ❧

ecorate the mantel with these special
stockings. "Friendly Santa" graph and instructions on page 127;
"Shadow Appliqué Stocking" instructions on page 128;
"Cutwork Stocking" instructions on page 130. 🔔 Pleated
grosgrain ribbon adds an opulent touch to a lush velvet scalloped
skirt. Simple to sew, it's a delight under the tree year after year.
"Ribbon Tree Skirt" instructions on page 131. 🔔

ransform a simple square of linen into a unique angel. This quick-to-stitch project is sure to be a favorite. "Winged Angel" instructions on page 132. ❧ Linen touched with Battenburg lace is folded into a dainty pocket for Christmas flowers. Hang it on a doorknob or on a drawer pull. "Battenburg Flower Pocket" instructions on page 133. ❧

Made by hand,

stitched with love,

given with pride

and received with

grateful

appreciation,

meaningful gifts

in the spirit

of the season.

GIFTS OF LOVE

𝒟rawn thread and a pinstitched hem on elegant linen – for breakfast in bed or tea with a friend. "Serviette for Scones" instructions on page 134. ❧ A cup of holiday cheer rests on an embroidered napkin. "Cocktail Napkin" instructions on page 137. ❧

Attach a Princess tape lace jabot to a favorite silk blouse for a Victorian touch. "Teardrop Jabot" instructions on page 139. ❧ Make your own lace fabric from fragments in your sewing basket. Add silk ribbon and pearl embellishments. "Lace Vest" instructions on page 142. ❧

*L*etter-writing becomes a pleasure when stationery is wrapped in an embroidered linen folder tied with silken ribbon. *"Stationery Folio"* instructions and embroidery design on page 144. ❧

ingerbread twins can be machine stitched or appliquéd on bibbed knickers or skirt. "Gingerbread Twins" instructions on page 146. ❧ Kitchen chores take on the holiday spirit when this jaunty snowman comes to life on a quick-to-stitch apron. "Frosty Apron" instructions on page 150. ❧

or Baby, or a beloved bear, this embroidered bib symbolizes the peace of the season. "Baby Dove Bib" instructions on page 151. ❧ Pintucks, Swiss beading, and puffing are trimmed with lace and placed atop a basket for keepsakes or stitching accessories. "French Handsewing Basket" instructions on page 152. ❧

*S*atin ribbon chocolates frosted with roses
and glass beads are tempting treats. "Ribbon Chocolates"
instructions on page 154. ❧ Personalize your gift giving with
handsome gift bags unique for each recipient. A festive array
of fabrics and embroideries make these bags as much fun to
make as to give. Instructions for all gift bags are on pages 155
through 170. ❧

Be
of Good Cheer

Seasons Greetings

JOY

CHILDREN AT CHRISTMAS

The magic of
Christmas
sparkles in the eyes
of children.
It's the occasion
for the ultimate in
holiday finery, the
dresses of our
dreams.

A smocked collar trimmed with lace adds drama to an elegant velveteen dress. "Smocked Round Collar" information on page 171. ✒ Shadow embroidery on an organdy jabot embellishes the neckline of a simple jacket. "Lace Jabot" instructions and design on page 172. ✒

hadow embroidery graces lace-edged batiste collars worn over velvet jumpsuits. ❧ Holly leaves and bows on collar are echoed on hem edges of delicate batiste dress. For more information, see "Shadow Work Designs" on page 174. ❧

A little drummer bear in duplicate
stitch is added to a purchased red sweater. "Bear-Rum-Pa-
Pum-Pum" design on page 174. ❧ Santa says "Shhh. Go to
sleep!" on this batiste collar edged with red ribbon. "Shadow
Work Santa" design on page 176. ❧

This purse masquerades as a gingerbread house that looks good enough to eat! "Gingerbread House" instructions on page 178. ❧ Smock plate is a variation of "Gingerbread Lane" by Lou Anne Lamar. Pattern for dress and jacket is "Just for Rosemary" by Becky B's. For more information on "Gingerbread Dress" see page 180. ❧

A Creative Needle Christmas 76

A taffeta Christmas tree is smocked and decorated on a black velveteen bodice. "Smocked Christmas Tree" instructions on page 181. ❧ Velveteen suspenders supported by Ultrasuede® holly leaves with covered-button berries are the focal point for a holiday blouse and pants. "Holly Leaves" instructions on page 182. ❧

Christmas is a time for holiday finery. The art of English smocking is the perfect embellishment for clothing, gifts and home accessories. "Room with a View" graph and instructions on page 183.

SMOCKING DESIGNS

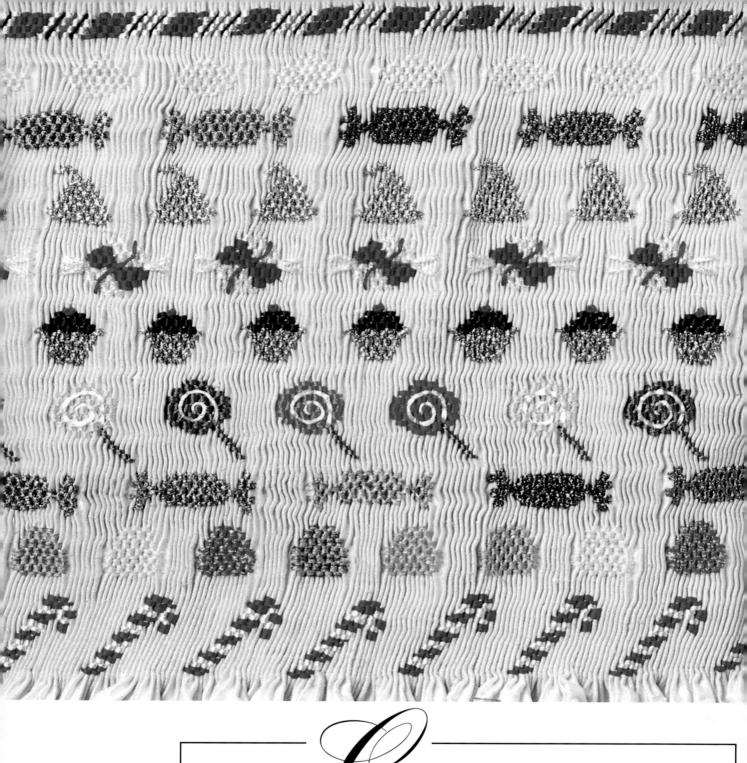

reamy silk edged with gold is the perfect canvas for lemon drops and lollipops, chocolate kisses and candy canes. Shimmering metallic threads lend a sparkling holiday look. "Christmas Candy" graph and instructions on page 185.

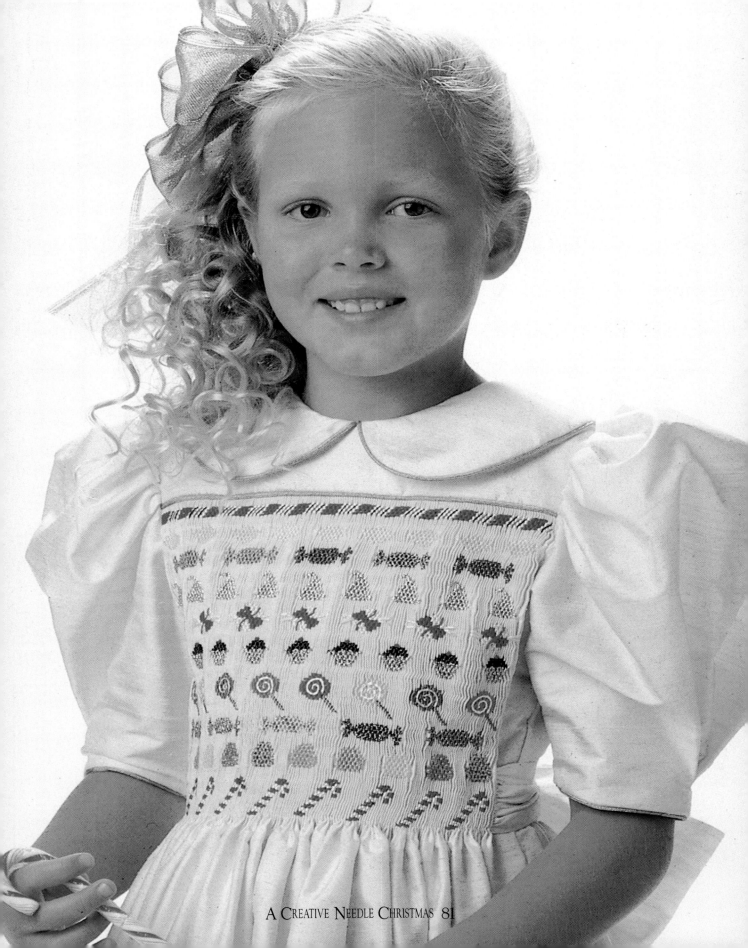

*V*ersatile "Merry Berry" graph is just as elegant on a baby bubble as it is on a holiday dress. "Merry Berry" graph on page 187. ❧ White silky broadcloth is an elegant and striking background for rich green holly leaves and shiny red berries.

From bedtime giggles to Christmas morning memories, this cozy nightie is just right when it's time for little ones to nestle in their beds. "Noel" graph and instructions on page 188. ❧ Cast a special glow at festive family gatherings dressed in Santa or snowman stars. "Christmas Star" and variation "Winter Star" graphs and instructions on pages 189 & 190. ❧

The splendid nutcracker dances into the season and into our hearts! Stitch this perennial Christmas visitor on a little boy's corduroy suit. Vivid primary colors add richness to a design destined to become your child's favorite. "Nutcracker" graph and instructions on page 191.

*R*ed velvet bows and shiny green holly – the colors of the holiday season decorate a lacy pinafore. It's a perfect finishing touch worn over a luxurious velvet dress. "Holly Bow" graph and instructions on page 193. ❧

Designed by Jennifer Crutcher

These patterns are adaptations from Belgian table linens. The designs shown are versatile and easily executed. Large spaces for filling make stitching easy for beginners.

Intermediate and advanced stitchers will find this a creative format in which to explore more intricate stitches. The needle lace stitches shown are suggestions only. They include Russian, single and double spider webs and double netting.

GENERAL DIRECTIONS

1. To make patterns for basting the tape, use non-fusible interfacing. Medium to heavy weight semi-transparent interfacing works best.

2. Trace the pattern from the back (wrong side).

3. Numbers indicate the order in which tapes are placed. The beginning point is indicated by an X and an O marks the end. The beginning point for basting the first tape is indicated by X-1; and O-1 marks the end.

4. Refer to the "Battenburg Stocking" for basic skills of basting the tape and techniques for needle lace stitches.

5. Picot tape can be used on any outside edge.

6. Since the stitching is done from the wrong side, always remember to turn the completed needle lace piece over when transferring it to fabric.

7. Wash and press after piece is completely finished.

PLACEMAT

Battenburg lace and placemat pattern on
  Pull-out
1 yd. linen or linen/cotton blend
  (enough for six placemats)
For each placemat:
  $1/4$ yd. interfacing
  $2 1/4$ yds. $3/8"$ tape
  $3 1/4$ yds. picot tape (optional)
  (If picot tape is not used, add yardage
  to $3/8"$ tape.)
Needle lace thread of preferred weight

1. Cut a 14" x 18" rectangle from the interfacing, making sure all the corners are at right angles.

2. Fold this in half lengthwise and then crosswise, creasing fold lines.

3. Trace the placemat pattern onto the interfacing, aligning the fold lines with the dotted lines on the pattern. The pattern represents only $1/4$ of the design. Trace the full pattern onto the interfacing. (For easier tracing, tape pattern to window or light table.)

4. Baste the tape onto the interfacing and fill spaces with desired needle lace stitches.

5. Make an oval pattern from paper or interfacing by following dotted lines on the edge of the pattern.

6. Using this pattern, cut out ovals from linen. (See diagram.)

7. Remove basting thread from interfacing to release the completed tape design.

8. Lift tape design, and with right side up, align onto fabric oval.

9. Baste tape to linen.

10. Attach tape to linen by hand using Turkish, half-Turkish or pin stitch. The tape may be attached by machine, using a satin stitch and a 50 or 60 weight thread.

11. Remove basting threads.

12. Using sharp scissors, cut away excess linen from behind tape.

13. Wash and press.

BUN HOLDER

Battenburg lace and bun holder pattern
  on Pull-out
12" square of interfacing
$1/3$ yd. linen
$5 1/4$ yds. $3/8"$ tape
$2 1/2$ yds. picot tape (If picot tape is not
  used, add yardage to $3/8"$ tape)
1 yd. narrow tape or ribbon, cut in half
  to make two ties
Needle lace thread

1. Transfer the complete design onto the interfacing. Half the design is shown.

2. Baste tapes and work needle lace stitches.

3. Make a circular pattern from paper or interfacing by following the dotted lines on pattern.

4. Using this pattern, cut two linen circles.

5. Edge each circle in tape, cutting away excess.

6. Place the right side of lace circle facing *down*. Put the two fabric circles on top of the lace with right side facing *up*. Pin 2" lengths of narrow tape or ribbon across the circle as indicated on pattern. The ties should cross the center of circle. Machine stitch down the center of tape or ribbon through all layers. Refer to diagram.

7. Narrow hem the ends of ties. Wash and press.

NAPKINS
Battenburg lace pattern on Pull-out

²/₃ yd. linen (makes six 12" napkins or eight 11" napkins)
For each napkin:
   2 yds. tape
   4¹/₂" square of interfacing
Needle lace thread

1. Trace only the corner pattern onto the interfacing.

2. Baste tapes one and two.

3. Work needle lace stitches.

4. Pull threads on the linen to use as cutting guides for the desired size napkin.

5. Lift completed tape design, and with right side up, align on linen square.

6. Baste motif and a length of tape along four sides, mitering each corner.

7. Attach tape to linen, using desired method.

8. Cut excess linen from behind motif and edging.

Embroidered Christmas Crackers *Shown on pages 11 & 14*

Designed by Carolyn Walker

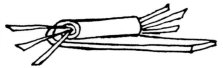

A sumptuous interpretation of the festive English tradition for holiday times, these crackers are embellished with embroidery, and ribbons, and will be treasured year after year. Such gifts as miniature bottles of perfume, cuff links, theatre tickets, or small toys are kept secret until a gentle tug on the knotted ribbon streamer reveals the surprise hidden in each cracker. What a wonderful tradition to begin now!

GENERAL INSTRUCTIONS
1. Finish decorative edges.

2. Work central motif, then dots, if any. *Note: When dots are included in a design, granitos have been used. A granito is a raised bump stitch, achieved by stitching six or seven times into the same holes, with a very firm tension. French knots or beads may be substituted. Anchor beads securely with a tiny, elongated cross stitches.*

3. Join long, unfinished edges with a French seam.

4. Place streamers (¹/₈" and ¹/₁₆" ribbons, cut 10" long) in center of a 3" x 18" piece of Pellon® fleece. Tack ribbons down, in a group at the center of one 3" end. Roll up, jelly-roll fashion. If a surprise is to be included, attach it to one end of a 5" piece of ribbon and tie a tiny knot on the other end for identification. Roll up surprise along with the ribbons.

5. Push ribbons and fleece through one

end of the embellished fabric tube, centering the fleece bundle. Tie with ribbon bows at each end of fabric tube, 1^1/$_2$" from finished edges.

CANDY CANE

Fabric: Blue cotton with white polka dots

Threads: Floche 349 red, 700 green, 702 med. yellow-green

Ribbons: ^{1}/$_2$ yd. white ^{3}/$_8$" ribbon for bows

1^1/$_2$ yd. ^{1}/$_8$" red and white polka dot ribbon

1^1/$_2$ yd. ^{1}/$_{16}$" white ribbon

Order of work and stitches:

Edge – ^{1}/$_4$" hem, pin stitch in red.

Cane – Appliqué cane in white linen or cotton; overstitch red stripes in a long satin stitch.

Holly leaves – Padded satin stitch in two shades of green in each leaf.

Holly Berries – red granitos or beads

POINSETTIA

Fabric: White Swiss batiste

Threads: Floche 666 red, 700 green, white

Lace: 10" of ^{1}/$_2$" wide edging

Ribbon: ^{1}/$_2$"yd. ^{3}/$_8$" red for bows; 2 yds. ^{1}/$_{16}$" green for streamers

Order of work and stitches:

Edge – ^{1}/$_2$" lace edging; pin stitch ^{1}/$_2$" from raw edge.

Flower, leaves and stem – Shadow work; leave flower center open.

Dots – White granitos

Center – Fill with seed pearls or white French knots. ❧

Pattern for Applique

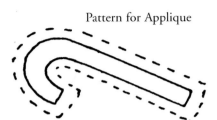

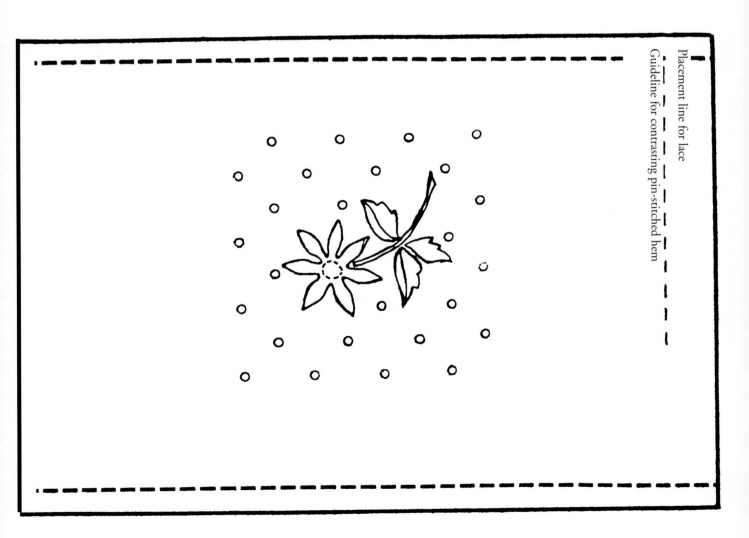

Placement line for lace

Guideline for contrasting pin-stitched hem

Designed by Janet Hierl

Combine the techniques of cutwork and appliqué to create these festive holiday accessories. Scraps of red and green linen are appliquéd to a white linen background. The base fabric is then removed or cut away. Since some dyed linens may not be colorfast, these projects are completed without the use of water soluble stabilizers or bonding materials. Test colorfastness of fabric as necessary. Add detached petals and leaves for dimension and interest. Then expand your machine stitching skills to include machine embroidered French knots. Complete your project with perfect tunnel-free satin stitched borders, or utilize your machine's hemstitching capabilities for a neat, professional finish.

FABRICS

Base fabric: white handkerchief linen or linen/cotton blend

Appliqué fabric: red and green handkerchief linen, ramie or natural fiber blend

FABRIC REQUIREMENTS AND LAYOUTS

For all projects, cut block of fabric and place right side down on pattern piece, positioning as indicated. Follow grainline markings exactly.

COCKTAIL NAPKINS

(Makes 4)

$1/3$ yd. 45" wide base fabric
10" x 14" block red fabric
Scraps of red and green fabric

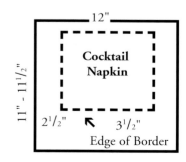

TABLE NAPKIN

(makes 2)

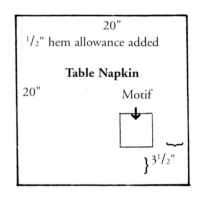

$3/4$ yd. base fabric
10" x 10" block of red fabric
Scraps of red and green fabric

PLACEMAT

(makes 2)

$7/8$ yd. base fabric
10" x 14" block of red fabric
10" x 10" block of green fabric
Scraps of red and green fabric

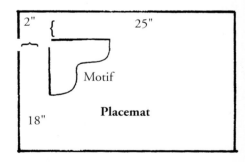

SUPPLIES

Placemat, napkin and template patterns on Pull-out
Open toe embroidery foot
Clear plastic presser foot
7" spring hoop
Appliqué scissors or small sharp scissors
Muslin padding ring

Sulky 40wt. rayon thread (red and green;
   yellow for embroidery highlights)
Fine white machine embroidery thread
   (optional)
No. 2 pencil
Dressmakers' chalk pencil
Seam sealant
#70 machine needles
Wing needle (optional)
Seam ripper or stiletto
Tweezers

PREPARATION
1. Press and lightly spray starch all fabric.

2. Transfer all design and cutting lines to the *wrong* side of the base (white linen) fabric using a No. 2 lead pencil.

Position the project motif according to pattern layout. Some projects contain detached leaves, and their position is indicated by a dashed line. Indicate leaf placement with a small X.

3. Trace detached portions of the design onto lightweight paper or interfacing. Cut out paper petal and leaf templates. Trace around each shape onto the appropriate blocks of red and green linen, using a white dressmakers' pencil.

4. Fill bobbins with red and green rayon thread. Embroidery highlights may be done using either yellow rayon thread or fine white embroidery thread in the bobbin.

5. Cut out 2 muslin padding rings. The inside diameter of these rings should be 1" smaller than the hoop and the outside diameter should be 1" larger than hoop. (A 7" spring hoop is recommended.)

SATIN STITCHED BORDERS
Thread machine and bobbin with green rayon thread. Use a #70 machine needle and a clear plastic presser foot. Engage the needle down option, if available. The hemstitched finish on the table napkin will be stitched after the cutwork.

1. Select a short, straight stitch. With the *wrong* side of fabric facing up, stitch around perimeter.

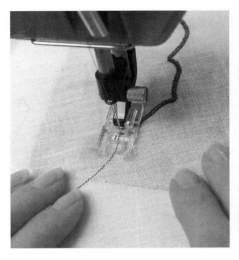

2. Set machine for appliqué or satin stitch. Satin stitches should lay smoothly side by side. The upper thread tension may need to be decreased to ensure that the bobbin thread lays under the fabric completely. Do not use too wide a stitch or tunneling may occur. Satin stitch over straight stitching with the *right* side of the fabric facing up. The right swing of the zigzag stitch should just clear the straight stitching line. Pivot fabric as needed for scallops.

CUTWORK APPLIQUE
For proper layering of the design motif, green leaves will be appliquéd first. Thread machine and bobbin with green rayon thread. Use a #70 machine needle and an open toe embroidery foot. A spring tension hoop should be used for ease in fabric manipulation. (Note: When stitching is completed or interrupted, always remove work from the spring tension hoop.) To create a firm stitching surface (and to protect base fabric), use two muslin padding rings.

1. Load 7" spring hoop on a flat surface as follows:
   a. Bottom plastic ring
   b. Muslin padding ring
   c. Base fabric (white linen) with *wrong* side facing up
   d. Muslin padding ring (optional)
   e. Metal tension ring

2. Position scraps of fabric to be appliquéd on right side of base fabric covering the appliqué area completely. Pin appliqué fabric in place.

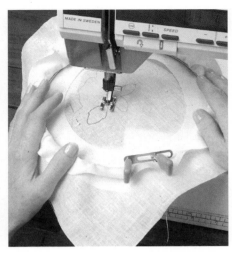

3. To secure appliquéd fabric and provide depth to the cutwork design, a padding stitch will be completed first. Select a short, narrow zigzag stitch. Pad stitch with wrong side up, around the area to be appliquéd. Reposition fabric in spring hoop as needed to complete all green leaves.

4. Apply seam sealant to padding stitches on the *wrong* side of fabric. Let dry completely. Remove project from spring hoop.

5. With appliqué scissors, trim the appliquéd fabric close to the padding stitch.

6. Turn fabric over. Carefully pierce the base fabric (white linen) with a seam ripper or stiletto. Trim from behind appliquéd fabric. (Do not cut appliquéd fabric.) Tweezers may be used to lift fabric as you trim.

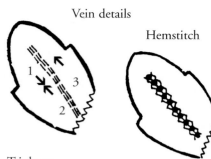

Vein details

Hemstitch

1   2   3

Triple or
Outline Stitch

7. Use the open toe foot and select a satin stitch or appliqué stitch. Load project in spring hoop as before with *right* side of fabric facing up. Satin stitch around all appliquéd leaves. The satin stitch should cover the padding stitches on the right side, and cover the trimmed edges of the appliquéd fabric on the wrong side. The areas where the appliquéd leaf fabric lays exactly next to a flower petal do not need to be satin stitched. The appliquéd petal will cover this portion of the leaf.

8. Leaf vein highlights may be outline stitched or hemstitched. To outline stitch, select a straight stitch length (1.5 - 2.5). Stitch vein detail to desired point, raise the presser foot, pivot with needle down, stitch along same stitching line to beginning point. Pivot again and stitch a total of three stitching lines. A hemstitch may also be used to stitch vein details. Insert a wing needle and select the desired hemstitch. Adjust stitch width and length settings as described.

STITCHING DETACHED LEAVES AND FLOWER PETALS

All projects contain detached flower petals, and some contain detached leaves. Thread machine and bobbin with the appropriate rayon thread. Use a #70 machine needle and open toe embroidery foot.

1. Load the spring tension hoop as follows:
   a. Plastic ring
   b. Muslin padding ring
   c. Fabric block with traced petals or leaves, *right* side of fabric facing up
   d. Muslin padding ring
   e. Metal tension ring

2. Pad-stitch (as before) along traced design lines.

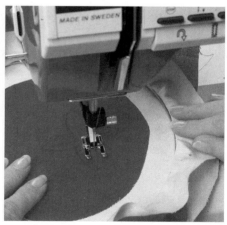

3. Satin stitch (as before) over padding stitches. Overlap beginning satin stitches to secure. To cleanly tie off ending threads, change stitch selection to a very short straight stitch (length 0.5).

Carefully reposition fabric, if needed, and stitch 3-4 straight stitches along edge of satin stitching. A bartack stitch may also be used alongside the satin stitching.

4. Stitch desired vein highlights.

5. Remove fabric from spring hoop. Press and lightly spray starch. With appliqué scissors, carefully cut out detached petals and leaves.

6. Position and pin detached leaves as indicated on pattern. Select a straight stitch and secure detached leaf by stitching on design line. Trim the excess leaf where it will overlap appliquéd flower petal.

CUTWORK APPLIQUED FLOWER PETALS

Appliqué the bottom layer of red flower petals in same manner as appliquéd green leaves. Trim base fabric. Satin stitch around trimmed appliquéd fabric. Use the tie-off stitch method to secure ending threads. Stitch petal veins as desired.

ATTACHING TOP SET OF FLOWER PETALS

The top set of flower petals will be attached to the project using machine embroidery French knots. Thread machine with yellow rayon thread. The bobbin may contain either the same yellow thread or fine white machine embroidery thread. Use a #70 machine needle and the open toe embroidery foot. Drop the feed dogs on the machine.

1. Position the top set of flower petals over appliquéd (bottom) set of flower

petals. Pin to hold in place.

2. To secure, bartack or stitch in place for 2-3 stitches. Clip beginning thread tail.

3. Select a zigzag stitch (width 1.5-2.0). Stitch 8 complete zigzag stitches. The top thread should form a small ball.

4. Change stitch selection to a straight stitch. Carefully lower the needle into the center of the ball and take 2 stitches.

5. Reposition the fabric and take one stitch in the fabric that just clears the ball of thread.

Reposition again to stitch in the center of thread ball. Again, reposition and stitch to the side of the thread ball, then back to the center of ball. To tie off, stitch again in the center of ball. Clip top thread close to ball. Gently tug the bobbin thread so that the tie-off stitch is on the underside of the fabric and clip. Repeat and add desired number of French knots.

MITERED CORNER AND HEMSTITCHED BORDER

To add the elegant look of a hemstitched border with neatly mitered corners, follow this easy technique.

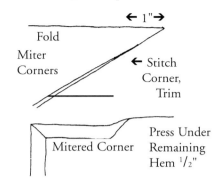

1. At the corners, fold sides *right* sides together to form a triangle. Select a short straight stitch (length 2.0) and stitch as indicated. Trim seam to $^1/_8$". Repeat for all corners.

2. Turn out mitered corners and fold up remaining edges at the $^1/_2$" hemline.

3. Insert a wing needle. Select desired machine hemstitch. Thread machine and bobbin with fine white machine embroidery thread. Use a clear plastic presser foot for greater visibility. The hemstitching should encase the cut edge of fabric on the wrong side. A lightweight tear-away stabilizer may be used to prevent puckering.

4. To complete the table napkin, miter and stitch the three corners ($^1/_2$" hem allowance has been added). Trim around appliquéd portion of napkin, leaving base fabric attached at the side edges. Trim to $^1/_2$" hem allowance. Press up hem allowance and hemstitch with desired stitch selection as above.

FINISHING

To complete projects containing satin stitched borders, press completed project. Trim excess fabric close to border stitching with appliqué scissors.

Shown on page 12 Festive Table Setting

Designed by Neal McQuinn

TABLE RUNNER

Yardage requirements for 13" x 32" runner

$^7/_8$ yd. 45" moiré faille, faille or cotton moiré

3 yds. decorative tapestry ribbon

14" x 33" piece of sew-in interfacing

1. Place right sides of runner fabric together. Place and pin interfacing to wrong side of runner fabric. With raw edges even, pin all 3 layers together.

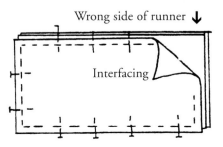

2. Stitch all 4 sides of runner with a $^1/_2$" seam allowance, leaving a 6" opening at one end. Clip corners; turn and press.

3. Start ribbon as shown, extending ribbon 1" beyond edge of runner.

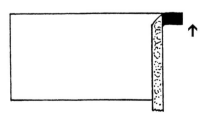

4. Pin ribbon to runner, keeping outside edges even.

5. At next corner, fold ribbon under at a 45-degree angle.

6. Bring ribbon back under 45-degree

fold, keeping outer edge of ribbon even with outside edge of runner.

Stitch diagonal folds.

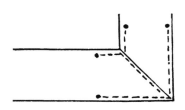

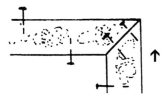

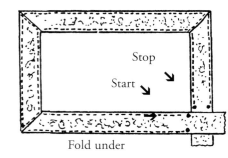

Fold under

7. Work same procedure for next two corners.

8. At the last corner, let ribbon extend over beginning ribbon. Pin in place. This corner will be worked after the ribbon is stitched in place.

9. Stitch $^1/_8$" inside edge of ribbon, starting and stopping where indicated and pivoting at corners. Stitch outside edge of ribbon in the same manner.

10. Remove pin at last corner. Fold under bottom ribbon even with outside edge of runner.

11. Turn top ribbon under, making a diagonal fold.

12. Stitch inside and outside corners and the diagonal fold.

NAPKIN RINGS

Yardage requirements for 4 napkin rings
1 yd. decorative ribbon
1 yd. lining ribbon
Cut decorative ribbon in 8" lengths, centering design.
Cut lining ribbon in 9" lengths.
Center decorative ribbon over lining ribbon and fuse together with Stitch Witchery®.

Fold with right sides together and stitch ends with 1" seam.

Trim decorative ribbon and one side only of lining ribbon to $^1/_4$".

Encase seam with lining ribbon and whip fold. 🍂

Christmas Tree Napkin *Shown on page 15*

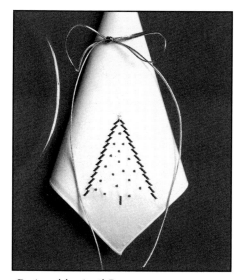

Designed by April Dunn

SUPPLIES *(for each napkin)*
Solid color napkin, purchased or hand made
1 spool each of red, green, brown and golden yellow 35-50wt. machine embroidery thread
Size 75/11 machine embroidery needle
Bobbin thread (Bobbinfil; Lingerie Bobbin Thread; Basting Bobbin Thread, etc.)
1-2 pieces 5" x 5" pin-on stabilizer (Stitch & Ditch; Totally Stable; Tear-Away, etc.)
Water soluble marker or pencil
Spray starch (optional)

FABRIC PREPARATION
1. Spray starch napkin to add more body (optional).

2. Place a napkin corner over tree pattern and trace design using a water soluble marker or pencil.

3. Pin stabilizer square(s) to wrong side of napkin corner, centering under markings.

MACHINE SET-UP
Thread for needle: Colored machine embroidery thread as indicated
Thread for bobbin: Bobbin thread
75/11 embroidery needle
Tension: 1-2 numbers lower than normal
Presser foot: Embroidery, appliqué or open-toe foot

INSTRUCTIONS
1. With green machine embroidery thread

in needle, select a stitch from stitch selection for the tree, or choose one of your own. Test on a scrap of fabric with stabilizer. Observe how the stitch forms and in what needle position the stitch begins to repeat. Adjust stitch width and length as desired.

2. Stitch over the angled "V" portion of design markings. If your presser foot has a center needle mark, align this with marked line.

Note: For some stitches (such as satin stitch or zigzag), begin at the bottom, stitch the tree to the top, pivot and continue back to bottom. Some other stitches (such as feather stitches) must be stitched from the tree top point down to bottom in order to appear correct.

3. Secure thread ends on wrong side of napkin or use a machine lock-off stitch.

4. Thread machine with brown thread. Select zigzag stitch. Adjust width to 2.5 and length to 0.3-0.4. Stitch base of tree as marked.

5. Thread machine with red thread. Select a period (.) from machine small alphabet. Test stitch and adjust width or length as needed. Select single motif/one time button or use while stitching, depending on the operation of your machine. Randomly stitch lights on the tree. If your machine does not have an alphabet function, use a narrow, short length zigzag, width 1.0, length 0.2.

6. Secure thread ends on wrong side of napkin or use a machine lock-off stitch.

7. Thread machine with golden yellow machine embroidery thread. Select a star or daisy stitch. Test stitch and adjust width or length as needed. Select the single motif/one time button or use while stitching, as before. Stitch selected design at the top point of the tree.

8. Carefully remove stabilizer from back of napkin. Press from wrong side. ❦

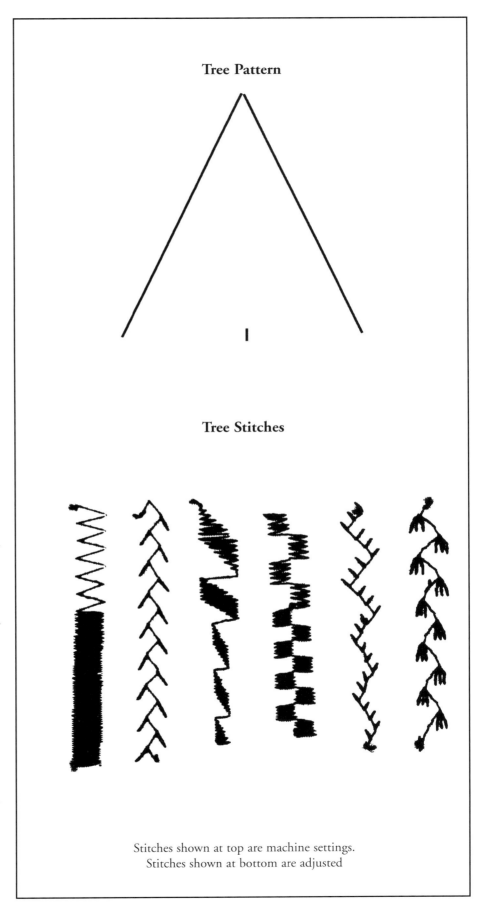

Tree Pattern

Tree Stitches

Stitches shown at top are machine settings.
Stitches shown at bottom are adjusted

Designed by Martha Parker

MATERIALS
(To complete three ornaments shown)
- $1/4$ yd. white batiste
- $1/4$ yd. white felt
- $1^1/2$ yds lace beading or insertion
- $1^1/2$ yds. $1/4$" ribbon
- $1/8$" ribbon (enough for ribbon bows)
- 3 yds. entredeux
- Embroidery floss
- 2", $2^1/2$", 3" Styrofoam® balls

EMBROIDERED PANELS
Trace the oval shape and embroidery designs onto fabric. Each ball requires four panels. Baste batiste ovals onto same-size white felt ovals and embroider. (The felt smooths the rough texture on the Styrofoam® and conceals thread tails.) Exception: Complete shadow work prior to basting to felt.

PUFFED PANELS
Using small stitches, gather along two sides, leaving ends loose.

Gather one side to 5".

Working on a piece of corrugated board or Styrofoam®, stab pin the ends of panel into felt.

Continue to pin, distributing gathers evenly along one side.

Repeat for other side.

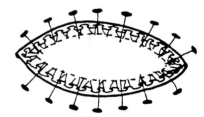

Cut on fold
(straight)

PUFF PANEL
Cut 2

Carefully remove pins from board. Pin gathered batiste to felt backing and baste in place.

ATTACHING BATISTE TO BALLS
Pin the four panels to ball, with sides almost touching. Trim away any overlaps to avoid a bulky seam. Whip together, pulling tightly.

LACE BANDS

2" ball: Cut two 7" pieces of lace
2¹/₂" ball: Cut two 8¹/₂" pieces of lace
3" ball: Cut two 11" pieces of lace

Entredeux may be whipped to lace beading if desired. Ribbon may be tacked under, or woven into the lace beading.

Pin lace beading at top of ball. Stretch over seam and pin again. Repeat with other piece of lace. Tack beading onto ball. Add a ribbon bow, lace edging or flowers. ❧

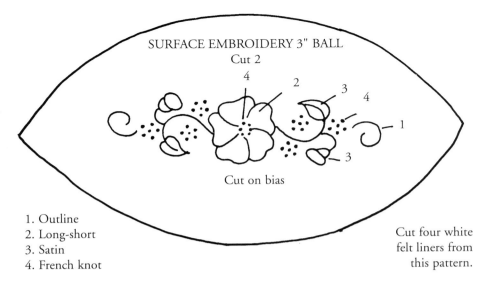

SURFACE EMBROIDERY 3" BALL
Cut 2

Cut on bias

Cut four white felt liners from this pattern.

1. Outline
2. Long-short
3. Satin
4. French knot

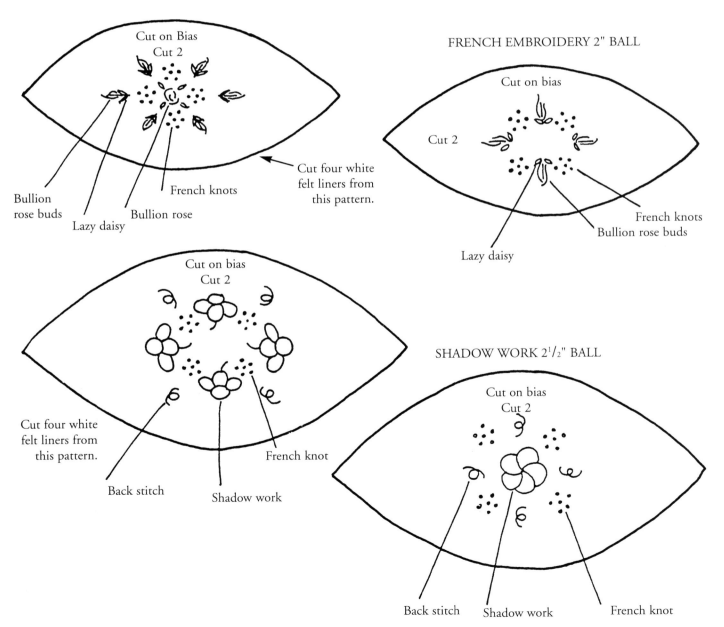

Cut on Bias
Cut 2

Cut four white felt liners from this pattern.

Bullion rose buds
Lazy daisy
Bullion rose
French knots

FRENCH EMBROIDERY 2" BALL

Cut on bias

Cut 2

Lazy daisy
French knots
Bullion rose buds

Cut on bias
Cut 2

Cut four white felt liners from this pattern.

Back stitch
Shadow work
French knot

SHADOW WORK 2¹/₂" BALL

Cut on bias
Cut 2

Back stitch
Shadow work
French knot

Designed by Martha Parker

MATERIALS

Fabric: Body/Bonnet
   $^1/_4$ yard batiste or linen
Lace:
   24" narrow edging for wings and collar
   18" narrow or wide for dress ruffle
8" narrow insertion
Ribbon:
   $2^1/_2$" ($^1/_{16}$") for sleeves
   2" ($^1/_4$") for hands
   3" ($^1/_8$") for neck bow
Polyester fiberfil
Assembly order: Body (including lace at hemline), lace collar, bonnet, sleeves, wings.

BODY

1. If desired, work embroidery at lower edge of dress. Stitch right sides together, leaving opening at top. Turn right side out. Tightly pack with fiberfil and stitch opening closed.

2. Gather and attach wide lace edging to one side of insertion. Right sides together, stitch ends, then overcast seam. Pull a thread in heading of insertion to make it fit curve at bottom of body. Pin and whip in place.

LACE COLLAR

3. Join ends of 6" of lace insertion, gather and whip to neck of body.

BONNET

4. Turn under front as indicated on pattern. Press. Pleat two rows. Using three strands floss, smock first row with cables. Work baby waves just under first row. Remove pleating threads.

5. Pin short ends, right sides together. Stitch $1^1/_4$" from back and $^1/_2$" from the front edges. Turn under back edge; run gathering stitches close to fold and pull tightly. Tack folds in place.

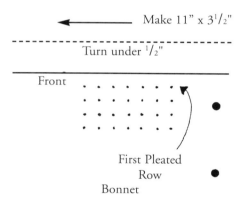

Make 11" x $3^1/_2$"

←

Turn under $^1/_2$"

Front

First Pleated
Row
Bonnet

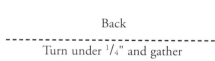

Back

Turn under $^1/_4$" and gather

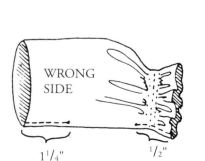

WRONG
SIDE

$1^1/_4$" $^1/_2$"

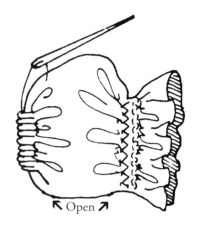

↖ Open ↗

6. Slip bonnet over head and tack down over top edge of lace collar. Cover the face by working a few stitches in the smocking and pulling tightly to form a face curve.

7. Add neck bow and tack in place to secure.

SLEEVE

8. Gather top of sleeve tightly with a running stitch $^1/_8$" from raw edge between the dots. Turn under close to stitching and secure gathers with a few stitches.

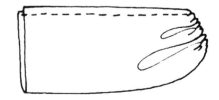

9. Right sides together, seam underarm. Finger press with seam centered.

10. Narrow hem wrist end. Turn right side out and pack with fiberfil up to wrist. Gather wrist with running stitches pulled tightly. Secure with a few back stitches.

HANDS

11. Tie knot in the middle of 2" piece of ribbon. Tack one end of ribbon over wrist gathers on seam side of sleeve.

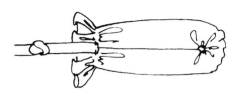

WRIST BAND

12. Whip $1/16$" ribbon over wrist gathers, having raw ends of this ribbon begin and end at underarm seam.

Repeat Steps 8 through 12 for remaining sleeve.

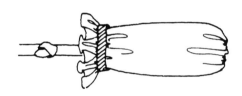

13. Place wrists together, underarm seams touching. Tack together with a few stitches. Wrist ribbons may be covered with embroidery or tiny pearls. Attach sleeves to each side of angel body with whipping stitches under sleeve top.

WINGS

14. Pull heading thread of narrow lace edging. Pin lace to paper wing pattern, adjusting gathers so lace will lie flat. Use one continuous piece of lace for both wings, twisting center so that scalloped edge will be on outside of both wings. Turn under and press raw ends.

15. Baste lace to paper with colored thread. For center circles, cut a 4" piece of narrow lace for each circle. Stitch ends together. Gather straight edge, pull tightly, and secure with a few stitches. Press flat. Pin and baste circles to paper pattern with colored thread.

16. With fine handsewing thread, whip

circles to inside edges of wings. With embroidery floss, work Russian filling stitch in spaces between circles and wings.

Twist at Center

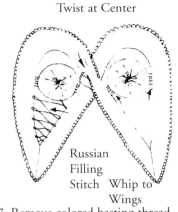

Russian Filling Stitch   Whip to Wings

17. Remove colored basting thread, stiffen wings with spray starch or weak solution of fabric stiffener. Allow to dry.

18. Whip wings to back of body. Wings will stand up if wings are pinched and stitched at base.

19. For hanging, attach ribbon or monofilament line to back of neck.

SUGGESTED EMBROIDERY FOR ANGEL DRESSES

Work feather stitch over heading of lace insertion. Buds are French knots. Leaves are turkey work.

LACE INSERTION

Work scallops in outline stitch. Roses are 3 bullion knots. Work fly stitch under each rose. Turkey work leaves accent scallops. ❧

Pattern pieces for Angel Body, Sleeve, and Wings are found on page 102. ❧

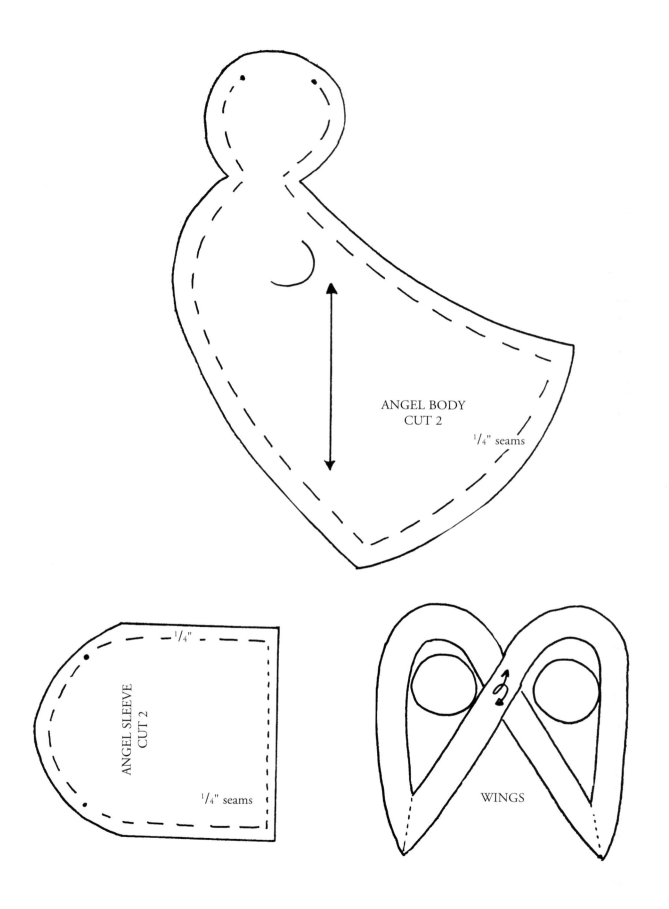

ANGEL BODY
CUT 2

1/4" seams

ANGEL SLEEVE
CUT 2

1/4"

1/4" seams

WINGS

Designed by Pam Sprinkle

MATERIALS

These materials are required for one ornament. See individual ornaments for extra materials needed to make specific ornaments.

Iron, scissors, compass, ruler, flexible craft glue, straight pins and pencil

Manila folder

$6^1/_2$ " square of #14 mesh needlepoint canvas

$^1/_3$ yd. fabric

Wonder Under® Transfer Fusing Web by Pellon®

$2^1/_2$ Styrofoam® cone

1 yd. of 1" wide or wider single-face satin ribbon for smocked band

$1^1/_2$ yards each of decorative cord or braid

INSTRUCTIONS

1. Follow the pattern (on Pull-out) and transfer the cone template to manila folder using ruler, compass and pencil. Cut out template.

2. Place template on needlepoint canvas and draw around shape. Cut out canvas.

3. Trace the template onto the paper backing of Wonder Under®; cut out shape. Trace a second template on Wonder Under®, this time adding $^1/_2$" seam allowance to all edges. Cut out.

4. Fuse Wonder Under® shapes to wrong side of two pieces of fabric according to manufacturer's instructions. Cut out the fused fabric shapes.

5. Peel paper backing from fabric shape with seam allowances. Place this fabric (coated side up) on ironing board and place canvas shape on top. Fold the seam allowances toward the inside of canvas and fuse in place. Ease in fullness around wide curve, miter corners and clip small inner curve to fit.

6. Trim $^1/_8$" from edges of remaining fabric shape. This is the cone lining fabric. Peel off the paper backing and fuse the lining fabric to the inside of the cone covering the canvas and folded-over seam allowances. Turn the shape over and press gently with iron.

NOTE: If making the corded cone, skip the next step.

7. Roll fused fabric into a cone shape over the Styrofoam® cone. Work with this until the shape is pleasing. (Cones shown in photograph overlap about 3" at the opening and $^1/_4$" at the bases. The diameters of the openings and bases are $2^3/_8$" and $^1/_2$" respectively.) Spread some craft glue on the overlap and press in place. Tack the fabric cone to the Styrofoam® shape with straight pins. Remove pins when glue is dry.

8. Glue decorative trims to fabric cone. Fold loose ends over the top of cone, or hide them in base opening. Secure these ends with craft glue. Attach ribbon or cord handle to cone with glue.

9. Wrap a piece of ribbon around the top opening $2^1/_2$ times. This is the amount of ribbon needed to pleat for smocked band. If the opening is 8" around, pleat a 20" piece of ribbon. Pleat 2 rows down the middle of ribbon, 1" wide or wider. Pull up gathering threads to 8" and tie off. Smock ribbon according to diagram.

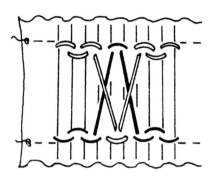

Basic Stitch: Cable/Wave Crossover

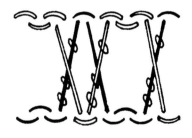

Bead Placement

10. Fold ribbon, with right sides together and raw ends even. Stitch ends together to create a circle of smocked ribbon. Remove gathering threads and glue ribbon to top of cone.

CORDED CONE

Follow steps 1-6 of instructions. Glue an embroidered piece of ribbon across the base end of flat cone. Roll fabric into a cone according to Step 7. Wrap 30" of cord around cone, tacking it in place with glue and straight pins as you wrap. Pleat 1½" and 1" wide pieces of ribbon together for top band. Smock through all thicknesses with DMC floss #503 (3 strands) and bronze glass seed beads.

CRAZY CONE

Glue gold braid over seamline and around base of cone. Use long gathering threads and pleat a 1" wide piece of grosgrain ribbon. Stretch ribbon to its full length and attach metallic lace, by hand or machine. Pull up gathering threads and tie off. Smock with red Kreinik braid (size 8). Sew an antique-type button to smocked ribbon. Attach smocked ribbon to cone, centering button over decorative braid. Thread gold ribbon under smocked stitches. Tie gold ribbon with overhand knots at sides of cone.

ROSE CONE

Smock with DMC Perle Cotton #8 in ecru on a piece of 1" wide picot-edge ribbon. Glue cord along each side of cone. Glue a cluster of fabric leaves at each side near top of cone. Attach smocked band to cone. Glue a ribbon rose on the band, near each leaf and one in the base opening. ❧

Santa-in-the-Moon *Shown on page 23*

By Pam Sprinkle

MATERIALS

Fabric: 4" x 35" silk pongee in slate blue
Threads: DMC floss in 326 red, 754 flesh, 334 blue; white, black and a color matching fabric for backsmocking.
Marlitt rayon floss 868 gold
Kreinik blending filament 002 gold and 032 pearl
Kreinik braid size 8 in 032 pearl
Small star-shaped gold sequins
Glass beads in metallic gold
½ yd. double-faced satin ribbon

2½" Styrofoam® ball
Straight pins
#8 crewel embroidery needle for smocking
Fray Check® and craft glue

FABRIC PREPARATION

1. Pleat 10 rows on 4" x 35" fabric; pull up gathering threads so pleated piece measures 4" x 8" and tie off.

2. Pull pleats together tightly, making sure they are straight and even. Block pleats with steam iron and apply Fray Check® to raw edges after pleats have set.

SMOCKING STEPS

Follow steps A-C on graph, working in order given. The design uses 46 pleats; 90 pleats are needed to cover a 2½" Styrofoam® ball.

A (Santa): Begin just above Row 4 and stack cables. Work down to boots. Use 3 strands of DMC floss unless directed otherwise.

Cap – DMC 326
Beard and hair – DMC white, plus one strand Kreinik blending filament 032
Face – DMC 754
Suit – DMC 326
Jacket Trim – DMC white

Gloves and Boots – DMC black
Face detail – Make straight stitches where indicated using DMC 334 for eyes, 326 for nose and white for mustache.
Sleeve trim – With 2 strands DMC white; stitch a 20-wrap bullion at each sleeve edge.
Tassle – With 2 strands DMC white, stitch a 4-wrap bullion at end of cap.

B (Moon): With 1 strand Marlitt 868 plus 1 strand Kreinik blending filament 002; work quarter-space waves to form moon.

C (Starry Night): With 1 strand Kreinik braid 032, stitch accents over 2 pleats in pattern shown on graph.

With 2 strands of floss, backsmock pleated piece with full-space wave stitches on Rows 2-9.

CONSTRUCTION

1. Remove gathering threads except for Rows 1 and 10.

2. With right side out, form fabric into a tube by matching 2 end pleats and Rows 1 and 10). Pin (if necessary) and slip stitch along seam formed by two end pleats.

3. Fit Styrofoam® ball inside tube. Draw up gathering threads tightly; knot to close tube ends over ball. On each gathered end, hide rough edges by pushing straight pins through fabric into ball. Seal ends with a dot of craft glue. Let dry and finish ends with woven spider webs.

SPIDER WEBS

1. With 1 strand Marlitt 868 floss, make web spokes by picking up pleats; insert needle under 2 pleats at a time. Draw thread through and pick up 2 pleats on opposite side. Pick up pleats for 6 spokes as shown.

2. After pleats have been picked up, slide needle under all web spokes. Loop thread around needle and pull up needle to form slip knot in center of web.

3. Make web by wrapping floss around each spoke. Hide thread ends in pleats.

STAR SEQUINS BACKGROUND

Put a bead and a sequin on a straight pin

and push it through fabric into ball. Repeat in a random pattern over background of design. 🐝

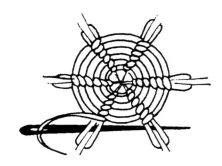

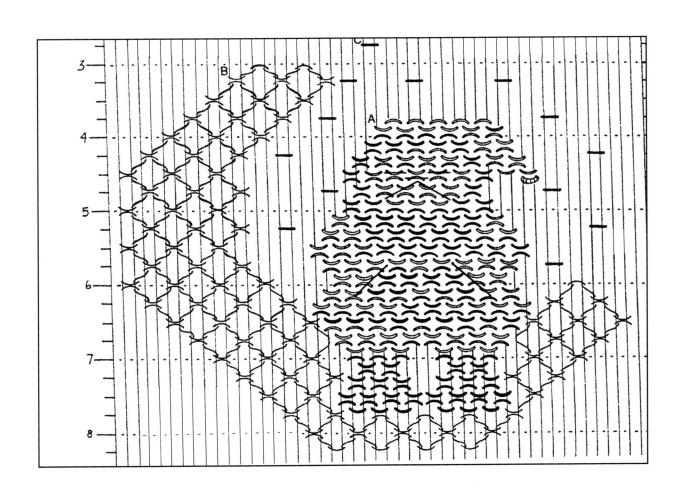

Designed by Martha Parker

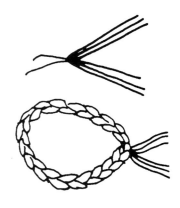

See Pattern Pull-out for Battenburg tape requirements and designs. For more information on Battenburg filling stitches, see "Battenburg Stocking" instructions on page 121.

ORNAMENTS

1. Trace individual patterns for easier handling when basting tape to design. Work is done on back of each design.

2. Pull the heavy thread on one side of tape to ease tape around curves.

3. Using contrasting thread, baste tape to pattern near outer edge, leaving enough tape at each end to turn back for neat finish.

4. Stitch edges of tape that touch with white extra fine thread.

5. Fill in spaces between basted tape with filler stitches, using your own or those suggested.

6. Clip and remove basting thread with tweezers. Starch. Press on towel.

ANGEL

Make arm and wing separately.

Basting order:
1. Apply tape to dress picot edge. Baste sleeve picot edge, and then wings.

2. Apply tape for dress sides and three bottom loops.

3. Apply folded strip of tape to two outer loops.

4. Apply last strip of tape to center loop.

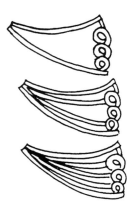

Head: Cut three 12" strands of floss; fold in half and tack at the fold. Braid, using two strands in each section. Secure again at end. Baste and attach to body as if it were tape.

Join taped edges and work filler stitches. Make a bar stitch across head and work buttonhole stitch over it (like a belt loop). Finish with a Russian stitch Juliet cap.

LINEN ANGEL

Assembly Order:
1. Make the halo, wings, and dress edge. Starch well.

2. Make the head and hair.

3. Make the dress following the general directions. Include a petticoat from paper or interfacing for additional support.

4. Insert the head and stitch in place.

5. Gather 9" of lace and sew on for collar.

6. Center arms over wings (back side up) and stitch in place.

7. Place wings on center of body and carefully stitch in place.

8. Bring hands together and tack at wrist. Put flowers in hands and stitch again. Attach a bow, knotting the ends of ribbon.

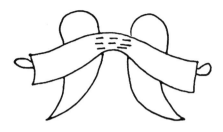

DRESS

Add seams for fabric pieces.

1. Follow the ornament directions to make the Battenburg lace edge, leaving $^1/_2$" extra tape at each end.

2. Pin the linen over pattern. Lightly pencil in embroidery designs. Pinning close together, pin the starched Battenburg onto the dress.

3. Remove from pattern and stitch Battenburg onto fabric.

4. Using one strand of 6-ply floss, embroider design.

5. Snip away excess linen.

6. Pin petticoat onto dress. Stitch neck hem. Then stitch center back seam. Turn. *(Note: To make pressing easier, stuff dress with a soft cloth.)*

SLEEVES & HAND

1. Trace the embroidery design and embroider. With right sides together, seam and turn. Add picot edge, starting at the top hand edge.

2. Trace and seam hands. Turn. Tack inside sleeves.

WINGS

1. Using instructions for ornaments, trace pattern for wings and baste tape to pattern. When wings are completed, starch well, and press on a towel.

HEAD/HAIR

1. Trace head pattern onto linen and seam. Turn. Stuff with polyfil.

2. Using filler thread, satin stitch head.

3. Using two threads, make French knot side curls.

4. Make coil curls by wrapping a 24" thread around a swizzle stick (knot end with regular thread). Invisibly stitch the length 4 times. Ease thread off stick, tucking loose ends inside curl with a toothpick. Make 4 curls. Fold in half and attach two whole curls to each side under French knot curls.

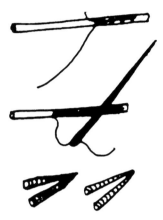

HALO

1. Cut three 9" pieces of filler thread.

2. Whip them together at one end and braid. Whip other end.

3. Starch, shaping into a circle.

4. Ease ends of halo under the hair and stitch.

Christian Symbols in Battenburg *Shown on page 26*

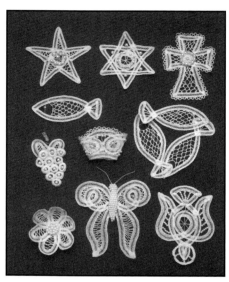

Designed by Martha Parker

Each ornament has its own special meaning. Additionally, the numbers (pearls, rings) are symbolic:

    One – One Lord
    Two – The two-fold Natures (Divine and Human) of God
    Three – The Trinity of Faith, Hope and Love
    Five – The Five Wounds of our Lord
    Six – The Six Attributes of God: Power, Wisdom, Majesty, Love, Mercy and Justice
    Eight – Regeneration through Baptism
    Twelve – The Apostles

Consult your favorite instructions for Battenburg filling stitches and general instructions on Battenburg, or see "Battenburg Christmas Stocking" instructions.

See each pattern for specific yardage and embellishment requirements. Beginning of each design is marked with "B." Illustrations show the back of ornaments. Press fusible interfacing directly to traced paper pattern to extend the life of pattern. After completing ornaments, heavily spray starch and press flat. Then add pearls. A pin will help hold loops in place while working.

STARS

Symbolism: Five points represent the star of Bethlehem. Six points stand for the six days of creation or the six attributes of God. The circle (no beginning or end) is eternity.

Directions: Make the center circles first. Five-point star uses eight (4mm) pearls. Six-point stars (two triangles) require 4 mm pearls in the points and 3mm on the circle. (See patterns 1 & 2.)

CROWN

Symbolism: "Be thou faithful unto death, and I will give thee a crown of life." Rev. 2:10.

Directions: Make the crown. Remove from pattern. (Optional: Whip princess tape or tiny tatting onto Battenburg circles.) Heavily spray starch. Add 2.5mm pearls. Join in the back. (See pattern 3.)

FISH

Symbolism: Early Christians would make this sign in the sand with their toe as a secret message to other Christians. Three fish joined in a triangle mean the Trinity.

Directions: Make a bar across the body. Work the scales (Point de Bruxelles) on this. For eye, use extra fine thread; put a loop around a 2.5mm pearl to hold it in place. (See pattern 4.)

BUTTERFLY

Symbolism: The larva represents our life on earth; the chrysalis, the grave; and the butterfly, our beautiful new life in the resurrection.

Directions: Baste the top of wings first, then the bottom. Cut three white felt bodies. Stitch two together and sew into the top of the butterfly. Starting at the tail tip, stitch on one 2.5mm pearl; then two increasing to four, letting them shape the body. Whip the third body onto the back for neatness. Add filler thread antennae. (See pattern 5.)

DOVE

Symbolism: The Holy Spirit descended as a dove at the baptism of Jesus.

Directions: Make the head-body-tail section first. Then do the wings and body loop. Nimbus (halo): Cut three 8" pieces of filler thread. Fold in half and braid, using two threads in each section. Baste as if it were tape. Pearls are 2.5mm. (See pattern 6.)

FLOWER

Symbolism: The creative power of God is shown in this symbol of the resurrection because the seed dies outwardly and is buried, and the inner soul will rise to glorious bloom.

Directions: Pin the completed flower onto a 2" Styrofoam® ball. Saturate with spray starch. Allow to dry. Remove and attach the completed center. Add a plain felt circle on the back for neatness.

Center: String twelve 3mm pearls into a circle. Whip this onto the edge of a felt circle. Bring needle through the felt and add six more pearls. Add a center pearl–3 or 4mm. (See pattern 7.)

GRAPES AND CROSS
Grapes
Symbolism: "I am the vine and ye are the branches." John 15:5. Fruits also refer to the bounty of God.

Directions: Cut twelve 30" pieces of filler thread. For eyelets, make 12 rings. Leaving about an inch tail, wrap the filler thread around a pencil ten times. Slide these loops to narrow end of pencil. Tape down thread tail. Buttonhole stitch over loops making a ring. Finish by tying the ends into a knot. Baste these eyelets onto the pattern. Then tack together, adding a 4mm pearl in the center of each grape.

Make leaves separately and add to the back. To make tendrils, wrap 6" filler thread around a swizzle stick or small straw. Stiffen with fabric stiffener or diluted white glue. Fold in half and tack onto back. (See patterns 8 & 9.)

Cross
Symbolism: The cross is a symbol of life's trials. It was the sacrifice of Jesus to give us salvation. The center circle denotes eternity with the outer ring of twelve pearls. The center pearl is our one Lord surrounded by eight stitches showing regeneration in baptism.

Directions: Begin Point de Bruxelles at the 4 ends of the cross and work toward the center. Cut two circles of white felt. Make a circle of twelve 4mm pearls. Whip around the edge of the felt. Put one pearl in the center and surround it with eight lazy daisy stitches, using three strands of thread. Add the completed center to the finished cross.

A pin will help hold the loops in place as you work. (See pattern 10.) ❧

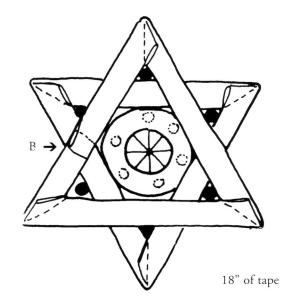

B →

18" of tape

Patterns 1 & 2

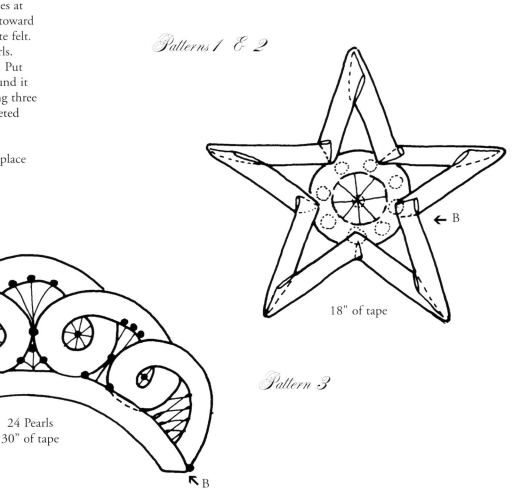

← B

18" of tape

Pattern 3

24 Pearls
30" of tape

Twist
Turn

↖ B

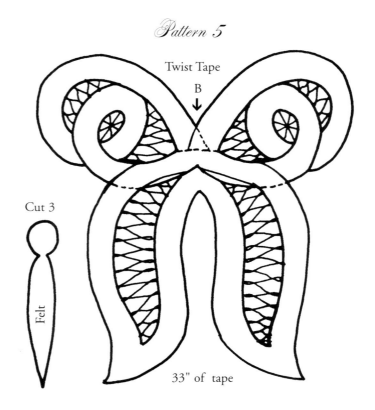

Pattern 5

Twist Tape

B

Cut 3

Felt

33" of tape

Pattern 4

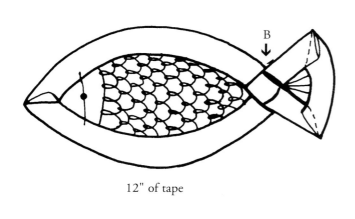

B

12" of tape

Pattern 6

B

36" of tape

Pattern 7

B

24" of tape

Pattern 8

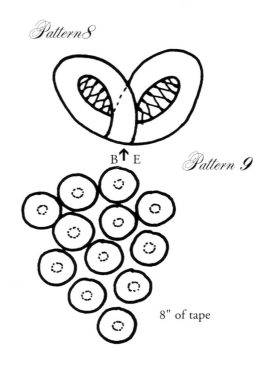

B ↑ E

Pattern 9

8" of tape

Pattern 10

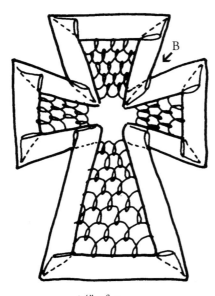

B

14" of tape

Sparkling Smocked Ornament Shown on page 28

Designed by Barbara Meger

This design is Series 5 of the Sparkling Smocked Ornament Ready-to-Smock Kits collection and is available in kit form from **Classic Creations.** See Resource Guide.

SUPPLIES
$4^1/_2$" x 22" lightweight acetate satin
Kreinik fine (#8) metallic braid (#393 is shown)
2" Styrofoam® ball
$^1/_2$" x 10" strip of paper
#5 or #7 darner or crewel embroidery needle

PREPARATION
Pleat satin with 11 full space rows. along the left-hand side of fabric, pull pleating threads out of fabric up to the first firm pleat. Take threads to the *back* and knot off in twos and threes near the thread ends. *Carefully* count off 80 pleats. Remove pleating threads from excess fabric on the right-hand side and tie off to the back as before. It is not necessary to tie off the threads to a specific width; leave plenty of room for working in the round later on (5" to $5^1/2$" is a good width). DO NOT TRIM EXCESS FABRIC. It may be helpful to run a contrasting color basting thread vertically down the peaks of pleats 1 and 80 to help identify them while stitching.

STITCHING
Follow design graph and begin stitching at **x** on Row $2^1/2$. Note that this is not a complete stitch. Just bring the thread out on the left side of first pleat and proceed to second pleat to continue moving down with a four-step trellis to Row $3^1/2$, cable stitch, and travel back up to row $2^1/2$ with a four-step trellis. End the sequence with a cable stitch. Work this design repeat *eight* times across the row, but do not stitch the final cable stitch of the last repeat yet.

At the end of the first row, after stitching 80 pleats, trim away excess fabric at each side to about $^1/_4$". Avoid cutting pleating threads and try to cut along a valley to prevent fabric edges from poking through seam later on. This seam will not be stitched. The smocking stitches will hold it together and the raw edges will fall to the back of the work once pleating threads are removed.

Join pleat 80 to pleat 1 with a cable stitch. Bring the left-hand side of the fabric around to meet the right-hand side so that pleat 1 is next to and to the right of pleat 80. Reach across from pleat 80 to pleat 1 to form the cable stitch. Pull this stitch tightly. Take the thread through to the back and tie off.

Following the graph, work remaining rows in the round with fabric held in a tube, reaching across from pleat 80 to pleat 1 on each row. It is easier and neater to start each row somewhere other than at the seam. Note that the stitch sequences at Row 6 in the center of the ornament are slightly different from the sequences at Rows 4 and 8.

FINISHING
The fabric must be trimmed to fit the ball precisely. Too much won't lie flat; too little leaves a large hole to cover. Since Styrofoam® balls vary in size, it is necessary to take an accurate measurement for each ornament.

Photo 1: Measure Styrofoam® ball.

Measure around the Styrofoam® ball using a small strip of paper (see Photo 1). Tear away excess paper and fold the measured length of paper in half. This equals the necessary fabric measurement. Hold the folded paper so that it is centered over the smocking design and note where the paper begins and ends. Carefully mark these points, by drawing lines on the fabric or using the extra pleating threads as reference (Photo 2). Use a needle threaded with a strong

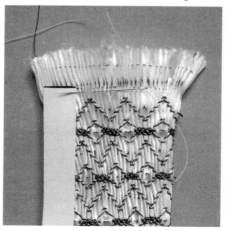

Photo 2: Fold measured paper strip in half; center over smocked design and mark above and below. Run a guide thread in fabric color $^1/_8$" above/below marked line.

thread (quilting thread or doubled regular sewing thread) in a color to match fabric. Stitch through all pleats slightly greater than $1/8$" to the inside of the marks (refer to Photo 2). These guide threads will be left in the fabric. Remove any remaining pleating threads and slide the ball into the smocked fabric tube. Cut off excess fabric at a point just above and just below the hand-stitched guide threads.

Photo 3: Remove all pleating threads; insert Styrofoam® ball into smocked fabric tube. Trim fabric along marked line, taking care not to cut guide threads.

There should be only a scant $1/8$" fabric remaining (see Photo 3). Pull up end guide threads as tightly as possible and tie off. Once tied, insert threads one at a time into a needle and take criss-cross stitches across the end openings (see Photo 4).

Photo 4: Draw up ends by tying guide threads tightly. Thread each guide thread into needle and take criss-cross stitches across opening to further draw up fabric.

Pull these stitches tightly to draw up the opening. Smooth down errant pleats with the eye of the needle. Knot thread to anchor; do not cut thread ends. Instead, run the needle through a pleat about a half-inch away and trim thread there.

COVERING THE HOLES
There are several alternatives for covering fabric ends on ornaments. The easiest is simply hiding them with ribbon loops, bows or roses, lace or eyelet poufs, buttons or faux jewels. However, it takes only a slight effort to elegantly finish a smocked ornament with woven or ribbed spider webs.

SPIDER WEBS
Spider webs need foundation threads or spokes for weaving. The number of foundation threads will depend upon the smocking stitches in the end rows. Cable stitches at the end of trellises or waves provide good anchoring points for spokes.

To lay spokes, knot a 30" length of same thread used to smock the ornament. Anchor thread with a backstitch in the center of area to be covered. Stitch through cable stitch immediately above center, then proceed straight down, passing over center and stitch through cable below. Use the eye of the needle so that the stitch is made only through the cable stitch and not the fabric (see Photo 5). Continue the stitch sequence around clockwise, returning to the center after the final spoke is laid.

Photo 5: For ribbed spider web, anchor thread in center and lay spokes by anchoring into cable stitches. Use eye of needle; do not catch fabric.

At this point, the spokes must be secured. At the center, make two or three back stitches, catching only spoke threads, to tie the intersecting threads together (see Photo 6). Do not cut thread. NOTE: If a thick thread, like metallic ribbon or ribbon floss, has been used, or if there are a large number of spokes, it may not be necessary to weave a spider web if all the fabric edges have been covered by the spokes.

Photo 6. After all spokes are laid, return to center to draw together all spokes using several back stitches.

An even number of spokes will require a ribbed spider web. Using thread anchored in the center of spokes and leading with the eye of the needle, so as not to pierce fabric or spokes, slide under two spokes counterclockwise and draw needle through. Now go back as if to make a back stitch over the second spoke and slide under that spoke and a new spoke next to it (see Photo 7).

Photo 7: Weave spider web by inserting needle under both an old spoke and a new spoke around and around. This causes a back stitch over the old spoke each time, which creates the rib.

Continue the sequence, over an old spoke and under the old spoke and a new spoke, around and around the center until all fabric edges have been covered, or until the spider web is as large as desired. To anchor thread, take a final back stitch over an old spoke and plunge needle into the ball through several pleats about 1" away. Trim thread close to fabric.

A woven spider web, with an uneven number if spokes, is begun in the same manner as a ribbed spider web. Use the eye of the needle and simply weave over and under the spokes until fabric edges are covered

HANGER LOOP

Attach a loop for hanging. Twisted cord, ribbon, monofilament thread or self-thread may be pinned or stitched into place. A neat and easy loop is made by cutting a 12" length of thread used for smocking. Fold length in half and tie an overhand knot about 2" from the folded end. This leaves two free thread ends that can be inserted into a needle and secured to the ornament with several back stitches. Anchor the thread ends as for ribbed spider webs.

Hanger loops are usually attached to the spider webs. However, to show off your perfect spider webs or to feature the smocked design, attach the loop half-way between the spider webs, as shown in color photograph. ✿

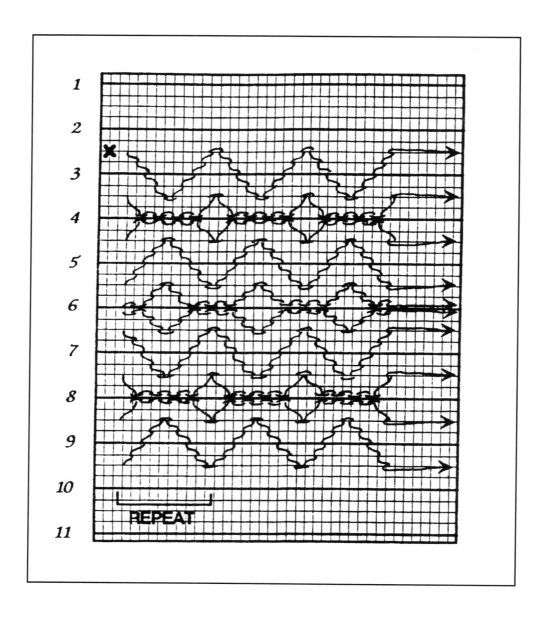

By Janelle Cox

MATERIALS
White Swiss batiste
White handkerchief linen
   (used as liner under batiste)
Mauve moiré
Mat board
Poster board
$1/4$" thick polyurethane foam
43" Kreinik's #8 Torsade twisted cord;
   Kreinik's Japan silver #1-001J for
   wrapping cord of tassels
Needles: #26 tapestry (shadow stitch)
   #7 between (all other embroidery)
$3^1/2$" spring tension hoop
Water soluble marker and No. 2 pencil
Tacky Glue®
Razor-type knife for cutting mat board

COLOR KEY
#1 - Kreinik blending filament, lustre
      silver 001 HL
#2 - White floche
#3 - 3689 light pink floche
#4 - 3688 dark pink floche
#5 - 815 cranberry floche
#6 - 991 dark green

STITCH KEY
A - Backstitch
B - Shadow stitch
C - Granitos
D - Satin Stitch

EMBROIDERY INSTRUCTIONS
1. Transfer embroidery designs to Swiss batiste with water soluble marker.

2. Baste 2" circle of white Swiss batiste on wrong side of marked batiste behind deer. Baste close to stitching lines.

3. With white floche and blending filament, stitch deer in backstitch, stitching through both fabric pieces.

4. Remove basting threads and trim batiste close to stitching from *wrong side* of design. (The fabric remaining creates a shadow of the deer when viewed from right side.)

5. Work shadow stitch for bow. (Use hoop for shadow stitch.)

6. Work granitos for bow center.

7. Backstitch leaves and pad the portion of leaf covered by satin stitch. Satin stitch leaves where indicated.

8. Work granitos for berries, and backstitch around granitos with Kreinik Hl Luster silver. Double thread for backstitching.

9. Stitch granitos for snowflakes.

10. Wash embroidered piece thoroughly, as well as batiste for back of ornament and linen fabrics, and press face down on towel. Spray starch.

ORNAMENT CONSTRUCTION
1. Using pattern guide, cut mat boards, poster board and all fabric pieces as indicated.

2. Transfer embroidery designs to moiré fabric with No. 2 pencil, marking lightly. Work embroidery stitches to cover pencil marks, since they will not be removed by washing.

3. Glue polyurethane foam to one side of each mat circle. Cut foam from inner opening of picture frame mat.

4. The poster board circle acts as a spacer behind picture frame. Trim poster board $3/16$" smaller than mat board all around. Do not apply foam to poster board.

5. Glue fabrics to mats and poster board by applying thin bead of glue around back edge of each. Clip curves of fabric, wrap fabric to back and press edges firmly into glue. *Note: Use linen fabric as a liner for batiste. Glue linen onto two mats as indicated above, then apply batiste over it in the same manner. This produces a smoother look when batiste is applied. The moiré does not require a liner and is applied as above.*

6. Glue poster board spacer with moiré previously applied to unfinished side of back mat.

7. Cut 6" length of twisted cord for hanger.

8. Glue approximately $1/2$" of twisted cord at top center of unfinished sides of front and back ornament.

9. Glue unfinished sides of moiré and batiste mats together, leaving an opening at the bottom of the frame to slide in photo. Allow to dry thoroughly. (It may be necessary to weight with books while drying.)

10. Adhere twisted cord around crevice of outer edges. Tuck in cut ends of mat for photo and allow cut ends for embroidered front of ornament to extend at bottom for tassel.

11. Glue cord around picture opening, allowing ends to extend also.

12. Cut six 12" lengths of Japan silver cord. With all 6 threads, form a loop and wrap $1/4$" for top of tassel (see illustrations). After wrapping, place thread ends through loop. Pull and tighten loop until threads are tucked under wrapping. Trim wrapping threads closely. The threads forming tail of loop can be left long and incorporated into the tassel.
Repeat for inside tassel and wrapping for hanger. Trim all loose threads of wrapping on hanger.

13. Untwist cords for tassels. Dampen slightly to remove kinks; dry and trim evenly. 🐝

Wrapping Illustrations

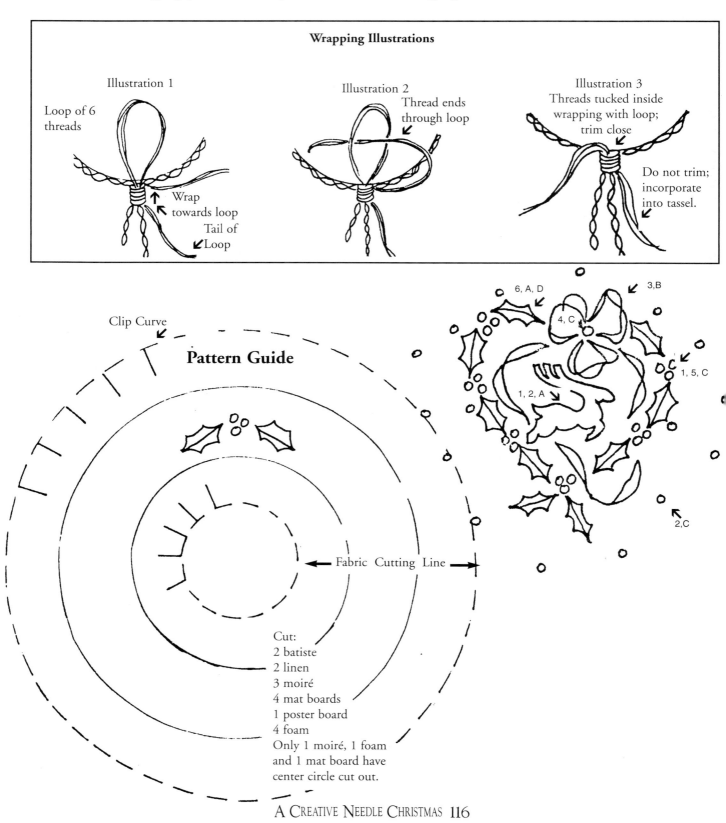

Illustration 1

Loop of 6 threads

Wrap towards loop
Tail of Loop

Illustration 2

Thread ends through loop

Illustration 3
Threads tucked inside wrapping with loop; trim close

Do not trim; incorporate into tassel.

Clip Curve

Pattern Guide

Fabric Cutting Line

Cut:
2 batiste
2 linen
3 moiré
4 mat boards
1 poster board
4 foam
Only 1 moiré, 1 foam and 1 mat board have center circle cut out.

6, A, D   3,B

4, C

1, 5, C

1, 2, A

2, C

Designed by Cassandra Dowling
Crazy patch instructions by Suzanne Sawko

A crazy patch project is by definition personally unique. So much of the construction and design is based on personal choice and the eye of the stitcher. Following are basic instructions to start you on the road to making your own work of art with the crazy patch technique.

Our duvet project contains 36 squares of crazy patch, joined in 6 rows of 6 squares each. It covers a queen-sized bed.

We selected $1^1/_2$ yds of 10 different fabrics, in widths from 45 inches to 60 inches. The central motif for each square is a five-sided piece of velvet (cut from a six-inch square of fabric). Half of the velvet pieces were embellished with lace or eyelet, and half with silk ribbon embroidery.

To make sure that each square of the duvet included each of the fabrics chosen, we divided each fabric piece into 36 rectangles. The sizes were varied, to assure a random look to each square. The fabrics were sorted into separate plastic bags which contained the embellished velveteen square, 10 rectangles and a 15-inch foundation square of muslin.

Squares are formed with fabric pieces in a varied pattern, and top stitched with feather or blanket stitching.

After each square was completed, a template was used to trim each square to twelve inches. Squares were then joined with $^5/_8$" seam allowances. Embellishment feather and blanket stitches were added along each seam line.

To form a duvet cover, stitch backing in desired fabric (we used velveteen) on three sides, and insert zipper for opening in one end. For an alternate method, backing may be added in two overlapping pieces with a button closure.

General Instructions for Crazy Patch Blocks

1. Spray starch and press foundation block. Cut center scrap with five uneven edges. Center it on block or place it a little off center for variety

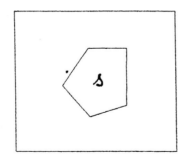

2. Place first scrap to center scrap, right sides together and along one edge of center scrap. Trim seams to about $^1/_4$".

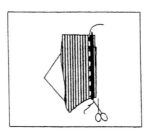

3. Flip scrap and press. Working clockwise or counterclockwise, add the next scrap along the next edge of center scrap. Trim away ALL excess seam to about $^1/_4$".

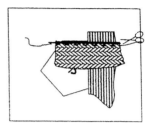

4. Continue around first scrap in the same direction, adding a scrap to each edge, trimming and pressing. When the first round is completed, cut all new angled edges.

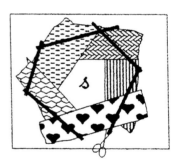

5. The second round of scraps is applied just like the first, and then new angled edges cut. Follow this procedure to construct subsequent rounds.

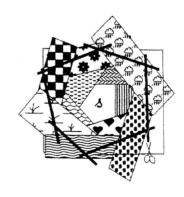

6. To break away from the concentric appearance, construct a fan. To create this look, sew, trim, flip and press a scrap along one raw edge of constructed piece. With a pencil, place a dot on the scrap at the point you want to develop the acute angles of the fan. Place a dot on the next scrap; match the two dots and angle next scrap as pictured.

7. When the foundation block is covered, press flat on wrong side, using a towel so as not to flatten embroidery. 🦋

 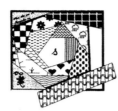  

Christmas Swan Tree Skirt *Shown on page 36*

Designed by Janet Hierl

SUPPLIES

Pattern on Pull-out
5 yds. cream Ultrasuede®
$1/2$ yd. white Facile®
Scraps of black Facile® and dark green Ultrasuede® or Facile®
40wt. rayon machine embroidery thread to match white, black and green fabric
40wt. red rayon machine embroidery thread
Gold metallic machine embroidery thread
Regular sewing thread to match cream fabric

Nylon thread
4-ply gold lamé (Madeira Ltd.)
#90/14 ballpoint sewing machine needle
#80/12 universal sewing machine needle
Pellon Wonder-Under® Transfer Web
Pellon fusible or regular fleece
Pellon fusible web (optional)
Totally Stable iron-on stabilizer
$1/8$" Dritz basting tape
$1/2$" double-folded bias tape (ecru)
$2^1/2$ yds. $1/4$" ecru satin ribbon
6-0 glass beads in ruby and cornflower blue
Hand-sewing needle and thread to match glass beads
Tapestry needle
Fray-Check® or seam sealant
Washable blue fabric marking pen
Clear plastic machine embroidery foot
Adhesive Teflon® strips for presser foot or Needle-Lube®
7-hole cording foot
Pattern weights (optional)
Press cloth

INSTRUCTIONS

Preparation

1. The tree skirt is prepared in five individual sections. Using the skirt pattern piece, trace the center opening and scalloped skirt edge onto *right* side of cream fabric. Cut skirt out along side edge. Flip pattern over, repositioning along center fold line; trace remaining half of tree skirt and cut along opposite side edge. Cut skirt sections around traced portions allowing approximately 1" margin.

Ultrasuede® Sewing Tip: Pattern weights may be used rather than pinning pattern to Ultrasuede® fabric. If pins are used, place them within the $1/2$" seam allowances. Additionally, skirt sections must be cut out with respect to nap. All skirt sections should be cut with fabric running in same direction. However, pattern may be rotated up to 45 degrees without affecting appearance of finished skirt.

2. Trace appliqué templates onto tissue paper. Templates have been reversed and are ready to use. Trace 5 of each swan body, beak and detached wing onto transfer web. Fuse traced appliqués onto *wrong* side of respective white and black fabric. Allow fabric to cool; cut out appliqués.

3. Body of swan contains 2 layers of padding. One layer extends up to beak of swan, while second layer is only in the main body portion of the swan. Place padding pattern piece onto non-fusible side of fleece. Cut out 5 of each layer of padding. Detached wing contains one padding layer. Cut out five padding layers from fusible fleece as above. If fusible fleece

is not available, trace padding layer templates as though they were appliqués, fuse to fleece and cut out.

Cutwork Holly Leaves

1. For the cutwork holly leaves, trace 30 leaves onto the transfer web. Fuse to *wrong* side of green fabric. Allow to cool and cut out. Remove paper backing and fuse the leaves onto the *wrong* side of another piece of green fabric.

2. Thread machine and load bobbin with matching rayon machine embroidery thread. Use the Teflon®-backed embroidery foot or apply Needle-Lube®. Stitch using either the #90/14 ballpoint needle or the #80/12 universal needle. Stitch vein highlights using a triple stitch (length 2.0-2.5) or straight stitch the same line 3 times. Satin stitch around the perimeter of holly leaf, pivoting carefully around points.

3. Cut out holly leaves close to satin stitching. Use appliqué or small scissors, holding the scissors at an angle to trim closely without clipping the stitching.

Appliquéing Skirt Sections

1. Peel off paper backing from each appliqué section. Position the padding layers under swan's body. Tuck beak under head of the swan and slip 2 holly leaves into place. Place the press cloth over appliqués, taking care not to shift them out of position. Fuse the swan in place. With tip of iron, press again around perimeter of swan to ensure a firm seal onto the skirt section.

2. On the *wrong* side of skirt, fuse stabilizer under area to be appliquéd.

3. Using washable blue fabric marker, mark feather details onto appliqué.

4. Load bobbin with regular sewing thread. Again, use Teflon®-backed machine embroidery foot or apply Needle-Lube®. Due to thickness of fabric and the addition of padding, to prevent skipped stitches, the #90/14 ballpoint needle must be used. Stitch the split of the beak using gold metallic embroidery thread (use triple stitch or 3 lines of straight stitching). Satin stitch the bump on beak, varying width of stitch to fill indicated area.

5. Satin stitch beak, then body of swan. Plan and stitch marked detail areas so that feathers appear to fall under adjacent feathers.

Couched Cord Embellishment

1. Couched threads or cords may be used to give more definition to appliqué designs. A number of machine stitches can be used to couch threads, including the zigzag stitch, the picot stitch and the blind hem stitch. Thread needle with nylon thread, using a 7-hole cording foot (or stitch-appropriate foot) to guide gold cord.

2. The couching stitch should just encase the cord, and is positioned along outer edge of appliqué satin stitching. Experiment with stitch selection and settings.

3. Thread a tapestry needle with ends of couched cording and push through to backside of work. Tie off cord with 2 overhand knots. Apply seam sealant to ends of cord to prevent fraying.

Detached Wing

1. Peel paper backing off detached wing. Place padding section of wing under top appliqué. Place on the *wrong* side of another piece of white fabric and fuse into place.

2. Mark feather details with blue marking pen. Satin stitch wing, beginning and ending where indicated on pattern.

3. Cut out appliquéd wing. Couch gold 4-ply cord around outside of wing. Leave a generous tail of cord to complete the wing once it is secured to main swan body.

4. Position detached wing onto main body of swan. Complete the line of satin stitching, attaching wing to swan.

Complete couching the gold cord around the wing and tie off on the *wrong* side of work as described above. Tack top of wing by hand to top of body.

Completing the Project

1. Remove the fused stabilizer from behind appliqué work. Cut, piece and fuse under scalloped edge. Satin stitch the cutwork borders of each section of tree skirt using red rayon machine embroidery thread. Use the #80/12 universal needle to stitch a finer satin stitch. Trim excess fabric close to satin stitching.

2. Assemble individual sections of tree skirt by using a conventional seam. Run a strip of 1/8" basting tape down the side of one section of skirt, keeping tape out of 1/2" seam allowance. Remove paper backing. Position and "baste" taped section to adjacent section. Stitch sections together using regular sewing thread in both needle and bobbin. Carefully remove basting tape. Join all sections of tree skirt, leaving a back opening between sections 1 and 5.

3. Press all seams open. Cut narrow 1/4" strips of fusible web; position web under each seam allowance and fuse in place.

4. To provide a cleaner cutwork edge, couch 2 lengths of the 4-ply gold cord to entire bottom edge of skirt.

5. Finish top opening of skirt with bias tape. Trim top opening along cutting line. Steam press bias tape into a circle. Stitch *right* side of tape to the *right* side of skirt using a 1/2" seam.

The edge of bias tape will be 1/4" in from the cut edge of the skirt. Trim seam to 1/4", clip curves. Press bias tape to *wrong* side of the skirt and topstitch in place.

6. Fold in 1/2" seam allowance along each back opening. Topstitch in place.

7. Cut the 1/4" ribbon into six 15" lengths. Attach 3 sets of ties, evenly spaced, down the back opening.

8. Arrange the remaining holly leaves around the neck of the swans. Tack into place and attach red glass beads as holly berries. For eye, attach a blue glass bead.

9. Remove blue pen lines with cold water.

Ultrasuede® Tip
To care for Ultrasuede® projects, machine wash in cold water using mild soap. Tumble dry on low heat. Dry cleaning white Ultrasuede® products is not recommended by the manufacturer. All colors of Ultrasuede® are completely colorfast. ❧

Designed by T. Lu Nixon

SUPPLIES

Stocking and Battenburg pattern on
  Pull-out
2 yds. 10mm embroidered tape
3 yds. 8mm plain tape
100% cotton thread #50, #60 for
  permanent stitches
Natesh 100% rayon embroidery
  thread
1/2 yd. moiré for stocking

INSTRUCTIONS FOR ASSEMBLY

Cut 2 stockings of moiré. Stitch with
right sides together. Clean finish top
edge of stocking. Turn down hem. Hem
by hand. Tack finished Battenburg lace
onto stocking according to design.

TRACING PATTERN

This pattern is a one-way design, which
must be traced, applied to fusible
interfacing, then worked. In order to
preserve the pattern for future use, trace
the pattern with a felt marker pen (a
pencil mark is too light) and tracing
paper. Place pattern, tracing side down
(so ink does not come off on tape), of

black fusible fabric. With a hot iron, fuse
the two together. Any weight fusible
material can be used. Black fusible fabric
is used because it is easier on the eyes. It
also stabilizes tracing paper after it is
crushed to make it more pliable.

APPLYING TAPE TO THE PATTERN

Measure and cut tape. Gather on one side
of tape, gently, until the center of the
tape is reached. On the same side of tape,
gather from other end. Do not cut the
gathering thread. Even on large pieces of
tape, the gathering thread can be pulled
up at intervals, then worked out to the
ends. If it is necessary to cut the
gathering threads once the lace is
finished, these threads must be knotted at
a crossing or overlap of the tape. They are
then whipped, and tucked between the
overlap, and secured. If the gathering
thread is ever lost, the lace is lost.

Place the tape on the pattern after the
gathering thread on the tape has been
pulled on one edge. Using no more than
5 short pins, pin the tape to the pattern
on the outside of tape. If 5 pins or fewer
are used, it is easier to prevent the basting
thread from being caught in them, and
they also prevent the tape from pulling
too tight or too loose. This can happen if
pins are placed too far ahead.

With pastel thread, begin basting with
1/8" to 1/4" stitches on the second loop.
Keep the first loop free in order that the
last loop can be basted. Always baste on
the outside of the curve and on the very
outside of the tape, placing the outside of
the tape right on the edge of design.
When basting, be sure that the two tapes
come close together so that they are
touching but not overlapping. Sometimes
the tape will overlap. The pattern will
dictate when this is done. Pull the tape
up with the gathering thread after basting
a loop and flatten the tape in center.

Continue to pin and baste.

TURNING CORNERS

Depending on the design, determine if
gathering thread is to move from one side
of tape to the other when making a
corner. To do this, pull the other side of
the tape to make next loop.

Straighten first gathering thread on the
unbasted end; then pull the second
gathering thread to form the next loop.

Keeping the gathering thread on the same
side when turning the corner can be
achieved by the way tape is folded.

Mitering makes a neat corner when the
tape comes to a right angle, or when the
corner cannot be under another tape as
part of the pattern. Place tape up one side
of square. Place a pin at the very point.
Baste up the outside, pulling the miter up
from the pattern, then baste down other
side. To make a sharp point, place an
extra basting stitch on each side of
corner, to hold it in place. When whip
stitching with matching cotton thread for
permanent stitching, fold the whole
pattern at the miter. Start at the inside
corner and backstitch to the point. Knot
stitch, fold miter flat on the square and
whip it down on both sides. Finish
basting, checking to make sure the loop
crossings overlap in the proper way. If the
crossing is changed, the design is
changed.

STITCHES

Russian Stitch

This is probably the most popular stitch
in Battenburg lace. Knot the thread on
the lower tape; then place the needle
through and under the upper tape (see
arrow), always keeping the thread in front
of the needle. Now pull the needle
through the lower tape. Stitches should
always be evenly placed with the bottom

stitches on the tape halfway between those on the upper tape.

Variation on Russian Stitch
After completing Russian stitch, bring thread back through. Work left to right. Work two buttonhole stitches on each side of figure eight of the Russian stitch. This makes the little ladder up the center.

English Wheel or Spider Web
Make a layout of crossed threads, stopping in the center of the fourth crossing. Knot the center together. Start weaving the needle under and over the spokes of the wheel to the desired size of the wheel. It is sometimes useful to change to a tapestry needle so the sharp point of a regular needle doesn't catch in the spokes. When the right size is reached, stop opposite the fourth spoke that was just taken to the center (thin line on diagram). Bring the thread through the completed wheel to the tape and secure at the tape. The wheel has to have an uneven number of spokes to weave (five, seven or nine spokes).

Rings
Wrap thread around a ring stick, a round object such as a pencil, or a finger, several times depending on the desired thickness of finished ring. Buttonhole stitches are then worked around the ring to cover it completely. The wrapped threads should be loose enough to allow the needle under the threads for overcasting. Remove ring from ring stick and finish off thread by passing needle through the buttonhole stitches on ring. The ring is now ready to be placed in the lace.

Rosette in Relief (worked from back)
This stitch is worked from the back, so it is executed differently than in embroidery. The rosette is similar to the wheel, except that it must have an even number of spokes and the stitch is raised on each spoke instead of woven. Lay out an even number of crossings. On the last one, wrap thread around it to the center; then knot center crossings together. Working from center, go over 2 threads or spokes; then back under and around. Pull thread gently so as not to distort the spokes. Continue until the desired size is reached by going over 2 threads and under 1, always coming up on the outside of the rosette. Knot last loop around last stitch before leaving rosette to go through center and wrap one of the spokes to secure at the tape.

Needle Weaving
Lay out pairs of bars. Depending on the size of the area to be covered, place one pair at the center of design, and pairs on each side. Weaving is started at smaller end and worked in heavier thread. Work out to width and length desired, then taper weaving by dropping outer bars one at a time. Push each weaving pass close to the preceding one with needle. Finish weaving on the two remaining threads, back to the tape, and secure. ❧

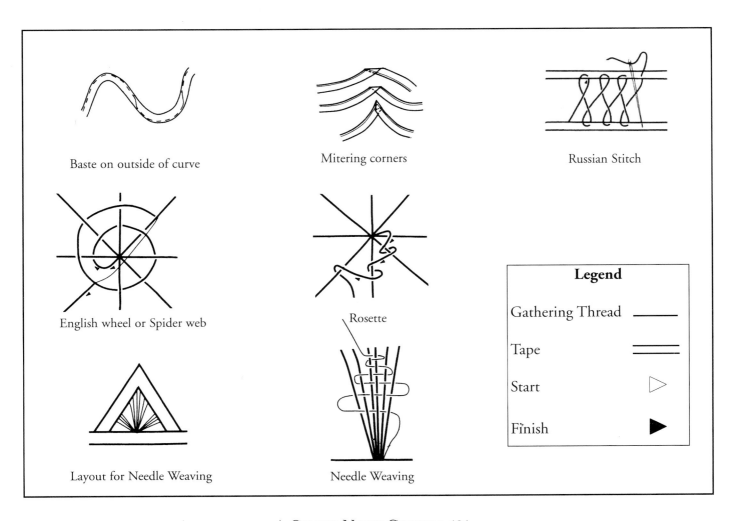

Baste on outside of curve

Mitering corners

Russian Stitch

English wheel or Spider web

Rosette

Layout for Needle Weaving

Needle Weaving

Legend

Gathering Thread ———

Tape ═══

Start ▷

Finish ▶

Designed by Martha Parker

Instructions are for embroidered angel with pearl-trimmed wings. Variations and additional materials for wings, halos, wreaths and embroidery follow.

SUPPLIES

Angel pattern and embroidery design on Pull-out

$1/3$ yd. of 45"-wide linen or batiste

#30 crochet cotton and/or 4-ply wool

$1^1/_2$ yds. of narrow lace edging (collar, sleeves, and skirt edge)

$1^1/_8$ yds. pearls-by-the-yard

1 yd. entredeux (optional)

Polyfil®

Embroidery floss

Small square of fusible interfacing for wings

Heavyweight paper or interfacing for freestanding angel (optional)

Head

Cut and seam head out of linen or batiste. Turn. Stuff with Polyfil®.

Hair

Using #30 crochet cotton or one ply of 4-ply wool, outline stitch the part in hair. Surface satin stitch in the natural hair growth direction. Comb to make threads look more even. Work side French knot curls using 4 strands of cotton or one ply of wool thread.

Halo

Tack ends of a 4" length of pearls-by-the-yard to back of head to form halo. Whip a small ribbon bow over joined area; tack to back of head.

Hands

Seam and turn. Polyfil® hand and forearm only. Stitch to upper body.

Wings

Trace design onto fabric. Embroider, using one strand of floss; clip tails. Trace and cut out second wings from heavy-weight fusible interfacing. Fuse to back of embroidered wings. Cut third set of wings for lining. Stitch lining wings to fused wings with right sides together. Wing lining can be similar or same fabric. Clip and turn. Close back opening. Press. Whip on prestrung pearls.

Dress/Sleeves

Trace design on skirt hem and sleeves. Embroider. Add entredeux to skirt hem and sleeve edge. Gather lace edging and whip to entredeux.

Joining sleeve to dress: With right sides together, sew sleeve to dress, beginning at neck edge and ending at notch on dress. With right sides together, seam sleeve and underarm as one, pivoting at previous stitching.

Turn back a tiny hem at the top of dress and sleeve and run a gathering thread. Pull tightly together and stitch onto upper body. Gather a 9" length of lace edging, and attach at neck for collar.

Make a paper or heavy Pellon® cone and pin to upper body, inside dress. This enables angel to be free-standing.

VARIATIONS

Embroidery: Use desired colors and thread for embroidered options shown on Pull-out.

Ribbon Wings: Cut one $8^1/_2$" length of $2^1/_2$" wide satin ribbon; fold in half and finger press a crease. Barely overlap raw edges, stitching in place.

Match center crease and seam; gather center of bow as tightly as possible, wrapping thread around gathers to secure.

Stitch wings onto the body to hold in place.

Silk Flowers, Leaves or Twigs: Pin

petals/leaves in desired position; tack in place. Twigs–Group small twigs which are approximately 6 or 7" in length. Hold together in center with narrow strip of tape and whip twigs to back of angel.

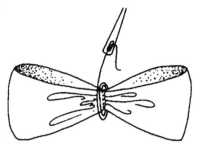

Ribbon Wings

Tack a small satin ribbon bow on top of twigs.

Halo: Join ends of a 4" length of jute, thread or cord to form halo. Whip a small ribbon bow over joined area; tack to back of head.

Wreath: Join ends of a 1¹/₃ yard length of ¹/₄" wide picot ribbon. Gather ribbon with long stitches, as in illustration, and pull up tightly to form a 4 - 5" circle. Whip gathers in place to secure. Add French knots, worked with six strands of floss, for holly berries or rose buds. Make

bow from a 10" length of narrow ribbon and tack to top of wreath. Whip angel's hands to wreath.

Other wreath options: Twisted jasmine vine or jute may be used. ❧

Ribbon Wreath

Snowbunnies Stocking *Shown on page 40*

Designed by Paris Bottman and Tina Lewis

SUPPLIES
Snowbunnies stocking pattern and embroidery design on Pull-out
1¹/₂ yds. lightweight white linen
1 yd. lightweight woven fusible interfacing
¹/₂ yd. fusible fleece

2 yds. forest green wool piping
Crystal seed beads
Red wool yarn tassel
Tiny silver jingle bells
DMC embroidery floss:
  310 – eyes, bunny head outlines
  Blanc neige – candy canes
  433 – snowshoes, sled ropes
  725 – sweater
  780 – sled, backpack, boots
  890 – trees, pants, tights, gift
  817 – gifts, foot straps, candy canes, hat, sled, scarf, mittens, boots
  797 – gifts, sweater design, skirt
  333 – gift, hat, mittens, sweater
  826 – gift, mouse shirt, hats
  3781– tree trunks
  318 – mouse
  899 – mouse suit
  963 – inner ears
  Silver metallic – gift ties, sled runners
  Gold metallic – backpack buckle, sled runners

INSTRUCTIONS
Trace three stocking shapes onto linen, adding ¹/₂" seam allowance. Cut. One

will be used for stocking back and two for stocking lining. (Fabric other than linen may be used for the lining.) Trace one stocking front with "Snowbunnies" design onto linen, adding ¹/₂" seam allowance.

Cut, leaving enough fabric to allow for an embroidery hoop. Cut one stocking of fusible fleece to back stocking front and one of interfacing to back stocking back. Cut 2 cuffs of linen, adding ¹/₂" seam allowance all around and leaving enough fabric around one to allow for a hoop to embroider name, if desired. The second one will serve as cuff lining. Cut 2 cuffs of interfacing.

Using a hoop, embroider "Snowbunnies" design, working from the right side. Candy canes are satin stitch. Snowshoes and sled ropes are chain stitch. Bunny heads are outlined with block backstitch. Trees are straight stitch. Sweaters are embellished with surface stitches.

Press and starch embroidered stocking

front, face down on a terrycloth towel. Cut out stocking front around seam allowance line. Fuse fleece to wrong side of finished stocking front. Add seed bead snow in a random pattern to stocking front.

Cover fleece with lining piece and baste. Using a zipper foot, stitch piping along stocking front seamline, clipping piping seam allowance at curves. Fuse interfacing to stocking back. Cover with lining piece and baste together. With right sides together, stitch piped stocking front to stocking back, stitching just inside line of previous piping stitches. Trim seam to $1/4$". Clip and notch curves. Serge or overcast seam.

For stocking loop, cut one linen piece 4"

x $1^1/2$". Fold long sides to center and fold again and edgestitch. Pin folded loop in place on wrong side of stocking back, just inside seamline of upper corner.

Embroider name on cuff, centering name on front half of cuff 1" above lower edge. Cut out cuff along seam allowance. Fuse interfacing to wrong side of embroidered cuff and to wrong side of cuff lining. Using a zipper foot, stitch piping to lower edge of embroidered cuff along seamline, clipping piping seam allowance along curve. Fold cuff at foldline right sides together and stitch short side seam. Press open. Fold cuff lining, right sides together, and stitch short side seam. Press open. Slip cuff over lining, right sides together, and pin together along lower edge. Stitch just inside line of previous

piping stitches. Trim seam to $1/4$". Notch curves.

Turn cuff right side out and baste upper edges together. With stocking inside out, pin right side of cuff to wrong side of stocking along upper edge, matching short cuff seam to stocking upper corner and easing in cuff fullness. Stitch, catching loop. Trim seam to $1/4$" and serge or overcast. Turn stocking right side out and turn cuff down over top seam.

Stitch bells to edge of cuff behind cording, spacing evenly. Stitch tassel to upper corner of cuff. See "Shadow Work Basics" for embroidery instructions. ❧

Victorian Christmas Stocking Shown on page 41

Designed by Esther Randall, YLI Corp.

Begin with small scraps of velvets, silks, woolens, taffetas, satins, and bits and pieces of lace.

Cut the pieces in various sizes and shapes. Start with fabrics as if doing strip quilting. Turn, cut and arrange the pieces for a crazy patch look. If adding embroidery embellishment, do not put a backing on patchwork. All embellishment is worked with YLI silk threads, ribbons and metallic threads.

Any embroidery stitch can be used with silk ribbon. (See "Hints on Using Silk Ribbon.") Add charms, beads, buttons, strings of pearls or bits of gold braid for added interest.

When embroidery is completed, cut out stocking. (See "Victorian Christmas Stocking" on Pattern Pull-out.) A thin layer of quilt batting may be placed between the patchwork and lining.

Stocking Assembly: Cut one lining and one stocking back ($2/3$ yard of satin or taffeta required). Cut one patchwork piece. Cut

one layer of light batting. Place batting to wrong side of patchwork stocking. Place right side of lining to right side of patchwork. Stitch across top. Clip seam if necessary, turn and finger press. Hem top of stocking back. Pin right side of stocking back to right side of patchwork stocking. Stitch around stocking shape. Trim, clip curves, turn.

Add pearls or braid, if desired, to outside edge of stocking. Add a ribbon bow and loop for hanging.

HINTS ON USING SILK RIBBON

To maintain a flat, untwisted appearance, used the outstretched finger, a bodkin or large blunt needle as a laying tool. The technique of "laying the stitch" involves bringing the needle up out of the fabric from the back, positioning the ribbon over the tool or finger, and holding the tool under the ribbon as you pull it down through the fabric. Do not pull taut. Any twist in the forward part of the threaded ribbon will be pulled through the material to the underside. Withdraw the laying tool or finger as the stitch is tightened.

To ensure the desired flat appearance, avoid knots. Pull the ribbon through fabric from back, leaving $1/2$" tail. Place the needle back down into the fabric to form the next stitch. Sew through the $1/2$" tail and continue stitching. In a like manner, knots aren't required at the end of ribbon lengths or stitches. Just trim ribbon close to fabric back.

The ribbon may look like it is splitting during stitching. This is normal. The creases will close when forming stitches. Be careful when stitching not to stitch into ribbon of previous stitches.

Keep in mind that dyes will have some effect on fullness of stitches. Adjust tension accordingly. 🦋

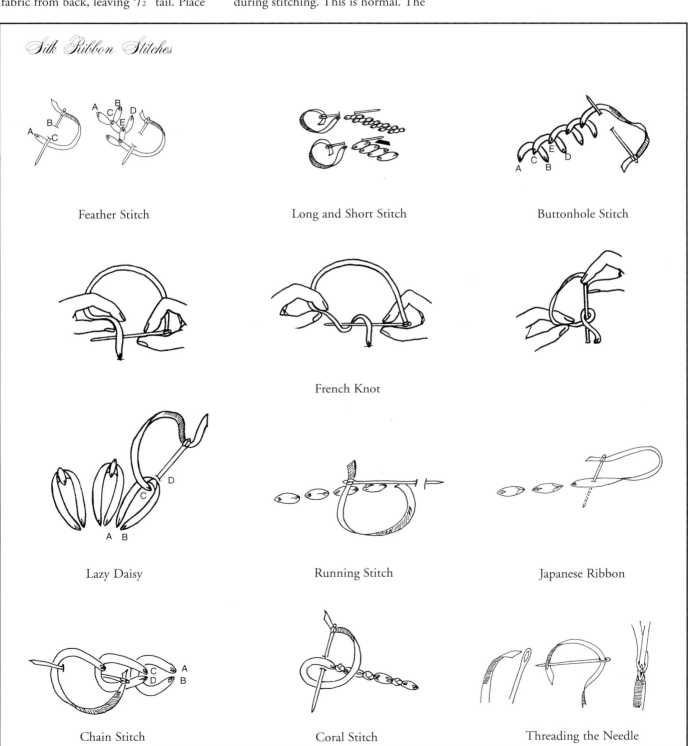

Silk Ribbon Stitches

Feather Stitch

Long and Short Stitch

Buttonhole Stitch

French Knot

Lazy Daisy

Running Stitch

Japanese Ribbon

Chain Stitch

Coral Stitch

Threading the Needle

Couched Rose

Ribbon Loop Stitch

Lazy Daisy Rose

Straight Stitch Rose

Fly Stitch

Chain Rose

Weaving

Satin Stitch

Leaf Stitch

Stem Stitch

Couching Stitch

Herringbone

French Knot Loop

Cross Stitch

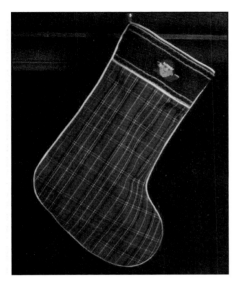

Designed by Hope Carr

SUPPLIES
Basic stocking pattern on Pull-out
1/3 yd. 45" plaid taffeta
1/3 yd. 45" lining fabric
1 3/4 yd. covered cording

SMOCKED INSET
Pleat a 5" x 45" width of fabric with 10 rows. Border is worked with cable rows and flowerettes on Rows 1and 2, and Rows 7 and 8. Background fill-in design is full space, 2-space waves with beads placed as desired. When smocking is completed, block piece to fit finished stocking width.

STOCKING
Measure finished smocked inset from top row to bottom row of smocking. Subtract this amount from stocking front pattern. Cut one stocking front (minus smocked cuff area) and one full stocking back from plaid taffeta. Cut 2 from lining material.

Baste covered cording (white taffeta is used here) as close as possible to bottom row of smocking. Stitch stocking front to corded edge of smocked cuff. Baste covered cording along outside edge of stocking front. With right sides together, stitch stocking back to stocking front along cording seamline. Trim seam allowance. Turn; press. Baste covered cording to upper edge of stocking. Baste ribbon loop in place at upper left back of stocking. Sew lining front to lining back, leaving a 4-inch opening along one side. Place stocking inside lining and stitch around upper edge on cording seamline. Trim seam allowance. Pull stocking through lining opening. Stitch opening in lining. Place lining inside stocking.

Mark center of fabric to be pleated. Pleat 10 rows (8 will be used in design). Santa requires 40 pleats. Use 4 strands of floss for stacked cables. Use 3 strands of floss for borders. Center Santa on fabric. Arrows on graph show direction of smocking.

BACKSMOCK
Backsmock rows 3, 4, 5, and 6 in thread which matches color of fabric.

SANTA'S CAP
1. Begin on Row 4, 13 pleats to left of center (black cable on graph). With red, cable 5. (French knots which form fur on cap will be worked later. Leave this area blank.)
2. Do not turn fabric. Working just above beginning cable toward right, with red, cable 20. Turn.
3. Cable 17; turn.
4. Cable 15; turn.
5. Cable 13; turn.
6. Cable 7.

SANTA'S HEAD AND SHOULDERS
1. Begin at left, just below beginning cable. With red, cable 3; with gray, cable 4; with flesh, cable 9; with gray, cable 4. Turn.
2. With gray, cable 6; with pink, cable 3; with flesh, cable 5; with pink, cable 3; with gray, cable 6. Turn.
3. With gray, cable 6; with pink, cable 4; with flesh, cable 2; with pink, cable 1; with flesh, cable 2; with pink, cable 4; with gray, cable 6. Turn.
4. With gray, cable 25. Turn.
5. With gray, cable 19.
6. Move 9 pleats to the right; turn. With red, cable 10; with gray, cable 17. Turn.
7. Move 5 pleats to left. With red, cable 5; with gray, cable 15; with red, cable 10. Turn.
8. With red, cable 10; with gray, cable 13; with red, cable 9. Turn.
9. With red, cable 13; with gray, cable 7; with red, cable 12.

SANTA'S ARM AND MITT
1. Begin on Row 5, to the right of Santa's beard, and just above shoulder. Working toward the left, with red, cable 8. Turn.
2. With red, cable 8. Turn.
3. With red, cable 8. Turn.
4. With white, cable 7 (cuff). Turn.
5. With black, cable 7. Turn.
6. With black, cable 9. Add 1 cable in black for thumb. Turn.
7. With black, cable 8. Turn.
8. With black, cable 7. Turn.
9. With black, cable 5.

FINISHING
1. Work French knots on cuff and fur on cap area.
2. Add tassle to cap by working feather stitch; snip off ends and fray. (Use 6 strands of floss for fullness.)
3. With blue, work French knot eyes. With red, work straight stitches for mouth.

Color Key:
Red   DMC 666
Gray   DMC 762
Pink   DMC 776
White   DMC white
Flesh   DMC 948
Green   DMC 910
Black   DMC 310

Graph and Legend on next page.

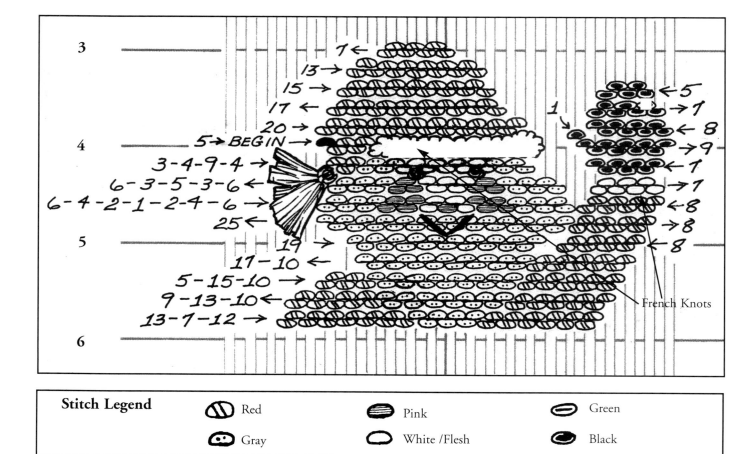

3

13 →
15 →
17 ←
20 →
7 ←

5 → BEGIN →

3-4-9-4 →
6-3-5-3-6 ←
6-4-2-1-2-4-6 →
25 ←

4

1 ↗

5 →
1 →
8 ←
9 →
1 ←
1 →
8 ←
8 →
8 ←

19 →
17-10 ←
5-15-10 →
9-13-10 ←
13-7-12 →

5

6

French Knots

Stitch Legend

Red		Pink		Green	
Gray		White /Flesh		Black	

Shadow Applique Stocking *Shown on page 42*

Designed by Kathy Albright

SUPPLIES

Shadow Appliqué design and stocking
  pattern on Pull-out
Finished size: 10" x 15"
Two pieces white felt, 11" x 17" each
Swiss cotton organdy, 11" x 17" each
Four 6" x 8" pieces solid cotton fabric
  for leaves: apple green, sea mist green,
  aqua green and forest green
4" x 4" piece cherry pink felt
$3/4$ yd. teal blue moiré taffeta for
  lining, backing and covered cording
One skein each DMC 6 ply embroidery
  floss: #501, #502, #503, and #992
  (leaves); #335 (berries and mouth);
  #632 (hair and face)
One spool each DMC silver and gold fil
  thread
30" piece $3/8$" wide teal blue satin
  ribbon

$1^3/4$ yd. $3/16$" diameter cording
100 Mill Hill glass beads, gold #557T
One spool ecru quilting thread for
  stitching beads
Standard $1/4$" single-hole punch to cut
  out berries
5" x 9" oval embroidery hoop
Air soluble fabric marker

INSTRUCTIONS

Trace and cut out stocking pattern,
adding $1/4$" seam allowance around
outside edge. Place stocking pattern onto
each 11" x 17" piece white felt. Cut out
two felt stocking shapes. Cut out one
stocking shape from organdy.

Position and pin organdy onto angel
pattern and trace angel with air soluble
fabric marker. Hand baste organdy with

traced angel to one white felt stocking. Insert organdy and felt stocking piece into 5" x 9" hoop, positioning angel design in hoop.

With two strands DMC 632 brown floss, embroider eyes, nose and hair using backstitch. Stitch through both organdy and felt. With two strands DMC 335, embroider mouth of angel using backstitch.

With one twisted 3-ply strand DMC gold fil thread, embroider wings of angel using stem stitch. With one strand DMC silver fil thread, embroider two curved lines on angel wings as indicated on pattern using stem stitch. Remove embroidered angel from hoop.

Trace and cut out the three leaf patterns. Place leaf patterns onto the four different shades of green cotton fabrics. Cut a total of 28 leaves, varying the patterns and fabrics. Do not add seam allowances. Referring to pattern for placement, arrange cut-out leaves and place onto felt stocking under cotton organdy. Remove hand-basted threads around outside edge of stocking as necessary.

With standard $1/4$" single hole punch, cut out 39 berries from cherry pink felt. Trim the fuzzy edges with small pointed scissors. Referring to pattern for placement, place and arrange berries onto felt and leaves and under organdy.

Hand baste leaves to felt stocking, stitching through organdy, leaves and felt.

Pin berries in place. With two strands embroidery floss, stitch around outside edges and down the middle of each leaf, using running stitch. Vary the four colors of green floss (DMC 501, 502, 503 and 992). Stitch through both organdy and white felt. Using two strands DMC 335 pink embroidery floss, stitch around outside edge of each berry using backstitch. Stitch through both organdy and white felt.

Referring to pattern, draw curved lines for vines onto organdy with air soluble fabric marker. With one 3-ply strand DMC gold fil thread, embroider golden vine, using backstitch. Referring to pattern for placement, hand stitch gold beads to surface of stocking using ecru quilting thread. Secure knots to back of felt.

From teal fabric, cut one bias strip 2" x 45" and a second strip 2" x 16". Strips may be pieced to form each length. Cut two pieces of cording, 16" and 45". Using zipper foot on sewing machine, wrap bias strip around each piece of cording, and machine stitch as close to cording as possible.

Place and pin 45" length covered cording to outside edges of sides and bottom of embellished stocking front. Machine stitch cording to stocking, stitching as close to cording as possible.

Using stocking pattern, cut out three stocking shapes from teal moiré taffeta, two for lining and one for back of

stocking. With wrong sides together, place and pin teal stocking backing onto second piece of white felt. Machine stitch the two pieces together, using $1/4$" seam allowance. The felt will stabilize the teal taffeta.

With right sides together, place and pin stocking front onto stocking back. Stitch as close to cording as possible, just inside previously stitched seams. Leave the top of stocking open. Trim seam allowance to $1/8$" and clip around curves. Turn stocking right side out.

Machine stitch 16" piece teal-covered cording around upper edge of stocking opening, overlapping ends of covered cording on back of stocking. Trim excess cording.

With right sides together, place, pin and machine stitch two taffeta lining pieces together, using $1/2$" seam allowance. Trim seam allowance to $1 1/8$". Insert lining into stocking. Turn top edge of lining toward inside to stocking. Hand stitch lining to stocking around upper edge of opening, just below the covered cording.

Holding one end of $3/8$" wide teal satin ribbon and fold three loops – small, medium and large. Hand-stitch loops together along sides with tiny whip stitches. Hand-stitch loops to one side of stocking. Repeat loop folding procedure on opposite end of ribbon. Hand stitch second set of loops to opposite side of stocking. ❧

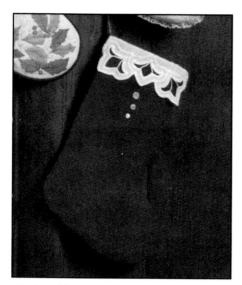

Designed by Rosemary Sandberg-Padden

SUPPLIES

Cutwork Stocking pattern on Pull-out
Anchor® pearl cotton No. 8 (10g ball)
  One ball: #1 White
Susan Bates® embroidery needle No. 4
White linen fabric, two 5$^1/_2$" x 10" pieces
Stocking fabric, two 12" x 17" pieces
Dressmaker's carbon paper
Tracing paper
Pearl buttons for trim, if desired
Finished mesurements (cutwork design
  only) 3" x 7$^1/_2$"

Trace cutwork design (see Pull-out) onto
tracing paper. Using dressmaker's carbon
paper, transfer design onto linen fabric.
Following chart, key and stitch
descriptions, work running stitches and
bars around design. Stitch blanket stitch
over all running stitches and bars. When
all stitching is complete, carefully cut
away areas indicated. Be sure all looped
edges of blanket stitches face areas to be
cut away.

FINISHING

Pin right sides of stocking fabric togther.

Stitch $^1/_2$" away from edges, easing at
corners. Trim seam allowance to $^1/_4$" away
from stitching, clipping corners as
needed. Turn right side out. Turn top
edges in $^1/_2$"; press and blindstitch.
Blindstitch cutwork cuffs to top of
stocking. Tack at sides.

STITCH GUIDE

Running Stitch
Pass needle over and under fabric,
making the upper stitches of equal
length. The under stitches should also be
of equal length, but half the size or less of
upper stitches.

Bar
Work running stitches along pattern
lines. At each bar, carry thread across
space, securing with small stitch behind
running stitch and back, then across
again, making 3 threads. Work blanket
stitch closely back over the 3 loose
threads without picking up any of the
fabric. All loops of the blanket stitch
must run in the same direction. After
working blanket stitch across bar,
continue running stitch along shape until
reaching the next bar. When all bars and
running stitches have been completed,
blanket stitch around shape.

Blanket Stitch
Bring thread out at the lower line, insert
needle in position in the upper line,
taking a straight downward stitch with
the thread under the needle point. Pull
the stitch to form a loop and repeat,
spacing the stitches closely together.
Note: The looped edge of the stitch must
face the area to be cut away. ❧

Key

——————— Bar
━━━━━━━ Blanket Stitch
▭▭▭▭▭ Cut away areas

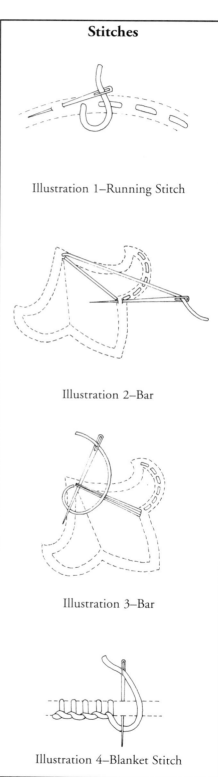

Stitches

Illustration 1–Running Stitch

Illustration 2–Bar

Illustration 3–Bar

Illustration 4–Blanket Stitch

Ribbon Tree Skirt

Designed by Lou Anne Lamar and Lucy Crosby

SUPPLIES
Ribbon Tree Skirt pattern on Pull-out
Short Skirt
1^1/$_2$ yds. of 45" or 50" fabric
3 yds. Pellon® stabilizer,
   #50 for heavyweight fabric

^{1}/$_3$ yd. Velcro®
16 yds 2" grosgrain ribbon (for pleating)
2^1/$_2$ yds. narrow ribbon (for seamlines)
2 yds. ribbon (for bows)
Matching thread

Long Skirt
2^1/$_4$ yds. of 54" fabric
OR
4^1/$_2$ yds. 45" fabric
4^1/$_2$ yds. Pellon® stabilizer,
   #50 for heavyweight fabric
18" Velcro®
20 yds. 2"grosgrain ribbon (for pleating)
3 yds. narrow ribbon (for seamlines)
2 yds. ribbon (for bows)
Matching thread

INSTRUCTIONS
1. Cut 6 scallops from desired fabric.
Note: If using velveteen or other napped fabric, cut all panels with nap in same direction. Cut 6 scallops from non-fusible interfacing. Baste interfacing to wrong side of fabric.

2. Cut 3 yards (2^1/$_4$ yds. for short skirt)

of ribbon for each panel. Pleat ribbon, using ribbon pleating guide included with pattern (on Pull-out).

3. With right sides together, sew pleated ribbon to skirt sections between dots as indicated on pattern. Turn and press.

4. Sew skirt sections together to form a circle, starting at top of section and ending at dot on pattern, keeping ribbon edges free, leaving back open. Finish seams with a zigzag stitch, or serge.

5. Center narrow ribbon over each seamline and stitch along both sides of ribbon.

6. Cut 1^3/$_4$ yds. ribbon for top edge. Pleat ribbon, stitch to skirt at top opening; turn and press.

7. Topstitch around skirt at bottom, and at top opening.

8. Finish skirt opening, adding Velcro® or ribbon ties for closure. ❧

Winged Angel Shown on page 44

Designed by Geri Frazier

SUPPLIES
Size 80/12 needle
Wing needle
Embroidery foot
12" square of 100% cotton organdy
8" x 4" rectangle of organdy
One 1" Styrofoam® ball
White rayon machine embroidery thread
Lightweight white thread in bobbin
12" length of $^1/_8$" or $^1/_{16}$" white ribbon
4" length of 2.5 mm pearls-by-the-yard
White fabric glue
Air soluble marker
   Note: Avoid blue markers, since the
   combination of starch and steam may
   cause the blue dye to wick into fabric.
   The iron may heat-set the blue line
   which may show through the stitching.
Seam sealant
Spray starch
One clip-type clothes pin

Set tension for machine embroidery for
all stitching.

INSTRUCTIONS
1. Spray starch and press each piece of
organdy two or three times. A very stiff
piece of fabric is needed, since no
stabilizers are being used.

2. Insert 80/12 needle in machine and
thread with rayon thread on top and
lightweight thread in the bobbin. Select
an elongated scallop stitch, or similar
stitch on your machine, and test stitch to
determine what adjustments are needed.

3. Find center of fabric square and mark it
with a pin. Draw a circle 10" in diameter.
Sew scallop stitch along this line.

4. Change to wing needle.

5. Mark a circle $^3/_4$" inside stitched scallop
and stitch a star shape or other decorative
stitch of your choice along this line.

6. Change to 80/12 needle. Mark a circle
$^3/_4$" inside star shape. If your machine is
programmable, select and program a
scroll/heart repeat pattern. Stitch around.

*Note: The piece probably looks a bit
buckled and drawn up; it will flatten once
it is pressed and starched again.*

7. Spray starch and press. Run a bead of
seam sealant along bottom of scallops on
wrong side of fabric to prevent clipped
threads from unraveling. Do not omit
this step. Let dry and carefully trim excess
fabric away along scallops.

WINGS
Use needle-down option to help
maneuver curves and pivots.

1. Draw wings on 8" x 2" organdy
rectangle.

2. With 80/12 needle, select a satin stitch
(length .02, width 4.4). Stitch around on
drawn line. *(Note: For best results, begin
stitching on bottom of wings, rather than at
a corner.)*

3. With wing needle, repeat stitch on
inner circle of angel body, reducing stitch
slightly in width and length. Starting at
bottom of wing, stitch around,
approximately $^3/_8$" inside satin stitch,

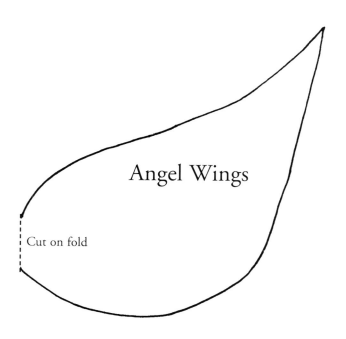

Angel Wings

Cut on fold

pivoting around curves and points.

4. Spray starch and press again. Run a bead of seam sealant along satin stitching on wrong side and allow to dry. Carefully trim away excess fabric.

ASSEMBLING ANGEL
1. Tie the 12" length of ribbon around center of wings, with knot at the front (right side). Center Styrofoam® ball on wrong side of fabric circle. Gather fabric under ball at neck and hold in place.

2. Place angel on wings, which are right side up. Bring ribbon around neck and tie into a knot. Bring ribbon to back, slipping under wings, and tie again.

Arrange folds of skirt so angel will stand.

3. With the 4" length of pearls, make a loop, and glue where ends intersect. Secure with a clothes pin until dry. Trim away tails of loop and glue pearl halo onto angel's head. 🍃

Shown on page 45

Battenburg Flower Pocket

Designed by Bev Moore

SUPPLIES
5"-7" Battenburg or crocheted doily
Lining fabric to match
Batting
Wood wool excelsior (or Spanish moss)
At least 4 types of dried or artificial flowers and greenery
$^{1}/_{2}$ yd. braided cord or ribbon for hanger
40" wired ribbon for a 7" looped bow
7" of floral wire
Hot glue gun, or Tacky® glue

INSTRUCTIONS
Pocket:
1. Most doilies are sheer and will require lining. If doily is embellished with lace around the edge, measure interior area and cut out a lining piece to fit, allowing $^{1}/_{2}$" seam allowance.

2. For pocket back, cut second piece same size adding an additional $1^{1}/_{4}$" along the top edge.

3. On lining, iron under $^{1}/_{2}$" along all edges.

4. On pocket, iron under $^{1}/_{2}$" along all edges; then fold over the top edge an additional $1^{1}/_{4}$" and press.

5. Pin right side of lining to wrong side of doily.

6. Pin wrong side of pocket to wrong side of lining.

7. Stitch down one side, across bottom and up other side connecting doily lining and pocket. Do not stitch across the top.

Stuffing pocket
1. Lightly stuff with batting in between the lining and pocket to $^{1}/_{2}$" from the top.

2. Glue ends of cord hanger to the inside of the pocket on each side.

3. Arrange flowers in hand, carefully gluing together at bottom. Keep adding flowers to create a fairly flat, wide arrangement that will fit in pocket. Place stems into the batting and glue in place.

Glue wood wool excelsior to the top of batting at the base of flowers.

4. Make looped bow with wired ribbon. Attach to floral wire or pick. Insert into arrangement and glue into place. 🍃

Designed by Susan Porter

MATERIALS

18" square linen cambric
DMC white embroidery floss
Fine white sewing thread
#10 and #12 crewel needle
#26 tapestry needle
Light-colored sewing thread
Embroidery hoop
Chalk marker
Stiletto

PREPARING FABRIC

Overcast raw edges of fabric on all four sides using fine sewing thread.

From the corner raw edge of material, measure $^3/_4$" to the right and mark edge with a small piece of colored sewing thread. Measure another $^3/_4$" to right and mark with colored thread. Move again $^3/_4$" to the right and place a third basting thread. Measure up from corner edge and repeat procedure. *Note: Fine linen cambric is not an even weave and no threads are counted. It is important to measure accurately on each side to assure a proper mitered corner.*

BASTING

Three basting threads are worked

horizontally and vertically across linen on all four sides. For a hem width of $^3/_4$", three basting rows are required for a correct hem.

Thread a #26 tapestry needle with pastel sewing thread. (A darker basting thread will leave residue on the linen.)

Use the mark thread as a reference beginning point. Baste across linen with sewing thread in valley between two fabric threads. (For easier stitch placement, score fabric by running point of needle along groove or valley, and gently pull linen.) Then stitch a few running stitches. Continue to score and baste until thread runs from one side of the material to the other. Baste all three lines on each side of corners. Also baste diagonal line. Notice the diagonal intersects all three vertical and horizontal basting lines. (See Illustration 1 at end of article.) Do not use knots; basting threads will be removed later. Complete basting rows on all corners.

TRANSFERRING DESIGN

Transfer design onto linen using a blue chalk marker sharpened to a very fine point. Draw design onto linen $1^1/_2$" away from intersection of the inside basting lines, using small, light sweeping strokes. When tracing small flowers, draw only a straight line to represent petals and leaves (see "Embroidery Design").

EYELET

Pierce fabric with stiletto, taking care not to break fabric threads. Thread a #10 crewel needle with one strand of floss. Hold thread against fabric with finger and catch the tail on back side while working first few stitches. Clip off tail thread. Continue to work eyelet around circle, pulling gently away from center and catching only two or three threads of fabric. Rotate the material to achieve a smooth, round eyelet. Bury thread by running under the overcast stitches on

back side. After eyelet is finished, use stiletto through the hole on backside to enlarge the hole on the front. For a finer look, use one-ply #150 cotton sewing thread.

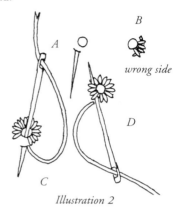

Illustration 2

SPLIT STITCH

Split stitch is worked on top of drawn line, and a hoop is used. This stitch is used to form a smooth outline around a design which will later be covered by the final satin stitching. Thread is split at bottom third of the stitch and pulled through; therefore, a soft thread is required. Results are similar to chain stitch. Refer to the number sequence in Illustration 3. Use a #10 crewel needle threaded with one strand of floss. Split stitch around the center section of pansy.

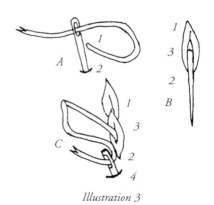

Illustration 3

SATIN STITCH

Work padded satin stitch as shown in

Illustration 4A - D, placing each layer of padding at a right angle to the previous one. Illustration 4D is the final step of padding, covering split stitch. In stitching final layer of padding, place first stitch just inside circle, slightly away from edge. It will dome and cover circle. If this stitch is placed too close to the edge, it will look more like an oval.

Always stab-stitch the padded satin stitch with fabric held taut in a hoop. The needle will go up and come down at an angle, tucking under split stitch. Observe needle placement along design to obtain a smooth edge.

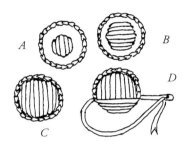

Illustration 4

MINI-PADDED SATIN STITCH

To pad a small leaf or petal, take a few running stitches inside leaf to secure thread. Sew two straight stitches. Stitch a lazy daisy.

Use one strand of floss and a #10 crewel needle. The lazy daisy may be eliminated if less padding is desired. The straight stitches used for padding flower petals may be placed in a turkey-track fashion.

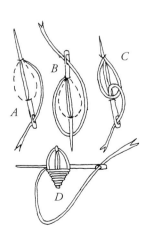

Illustration 5

TRAILING

Place embroidery in hoop. Anchor thread by placing a running stitch on traced line, or use an away waste knot. For trailing, couch with a closely worked satin stitch, using one strand of floss over a core of 5 threads.

For a finer appearance, use two, three or four threads as a core, but never just one thread. Pick up as little fabric as possible when couching. To achieve a smooth,

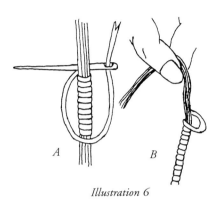

Illustration 6

even tension, pull core threads firmly every few stitches in a forward motion. (See Illustration 6A-B.) When approaching the end of a design, stop about $1/8$ - $1/4$" way, and decrease core underneath by sinking a core thread every other couching stitch. (To sink a core thread, thread a needle with one core thread, take it to the back of fabric, worked in a one-at-a-time staggered fashion.) At the very point of a sharp turn in trailing, one couching stitch covers twice the number of core threads. (Example: If core threads are 5, then corner stitch will be over 10 threads.)

When a leaf is positioned at the end of a branch, stitch leaf shape first with a lazy daisy stitch. Work branch with trailing technique. At the point where branch touches leaf, extend core threads of trailing into leaf for padding. Stitch final step of satin stitch for top layer of leaf.

DIAGONAL STEP STITCH

Sometimes referred to as rodi, this pulled thread stitch is worked diagonally down in two rows. Use it as a filling stitch inside the six background petals which have been outlined in trailing. Pull with a medium-tight tension, but do not pull

too tight when touching the trailing, as that will distort the smooth cord-like finish. When working inside a shaped area, center the step stitch diagonally across the middle of the design. Start at #1 and follow the number sequence, pulling the stitch after each step. The base of the stitch is up through fabric. Arrows point to where the needle

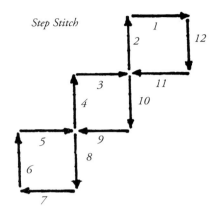

Step Stitch

Illustration 7

goes down into fabric. When opposite end of design is reached, take a traveling stitch right behind trailing.

Carry thread behind trailing so it will not show through to the front, and work up the next row. To avoid confusion, remember that when working diagonally down, the horizontal stitch goes from left to right and the vertical from south to north. When traveling diagonally up, the horizontal stitch goes from right to left, and the vertical from north to south.

DRAWN THREAD PATTERN

After the trailing has been worked around pansy shape, a drawn thread pattern is stitched on the center petal in the foreground.

Start in center of petal; cut two threads and withdraw threads back to trailing on wrong side. Cut away withdrawn threads within one thread of trailing. Skip next two threads. Cut and withdraw the next two. Continue cutting and withdrawing two threads in both directions.

Whip remaining threads together using fine white sewing thread. Work horizontal rows first, then vertical rows.

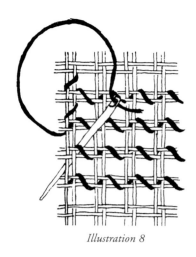

Illustration 8

FOLDING AND MITERING

After embroidery design is complete, remove overcasting stitches around edge of fabric. Turn fabric to wrong side.

Note: Practice cutting corner on graph before cutting fabric.

Fold along line A along basting thread and finger press into place, taking care not to pull or stretch linen. Fold and crease line C. Do same procedure on other side of fabric, sharply creasing fabric. Folds should form a perfect right angle.

Unfold two sides. Fold in diagonal line B, which will form a triangle. Crease and finger press firmly into place. Trim off excess linen. Refold lines A and C. Pin; baste hem and mitered corners.

PIN STITCH

Pin stitch is used for sewing two pieces of fabric together or to hold an appliqué or hem in place. The stitch resembles an antique hemstitch. The finished design creates a pattern or row of holes with the horizontal stitch slightly visible and the vertical stitch almost completely hidden.

Work pin stitch, using fine white sewing thread. Bury tail of thread inside hem fold about 1½" to left. Working on wrong side of fabric (next to right mitered corner), with the fold of hem facing away from body, move up four threads to left. Come to front of work. Slide needle under four threads to the back. Bring needle and thread out to front (Step A).

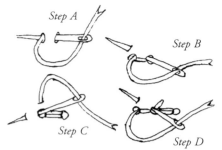

Step A *Step B* *Step C* *Step D*

Illustration 9

Repeat process, carrying needle diagonally under fold of hem. Pick up one or two threads of the fold (Step B). Pull thread tightly and repeat as shown in Steps C and D.

Continue working pin stitch across row until mitered corner is reached. Carry or weave sewing thread down to top of mitered corner.

Working diagonally up, blind stitch corner, picking up a thread on each side. Make sure that miter is secure at top of hem. Give fabric ¼ turn. Stitch next pinstitch row, and then mitered corner. Continue until all four sides and corners are complete. Remove all basting threads.

Embroidery Design

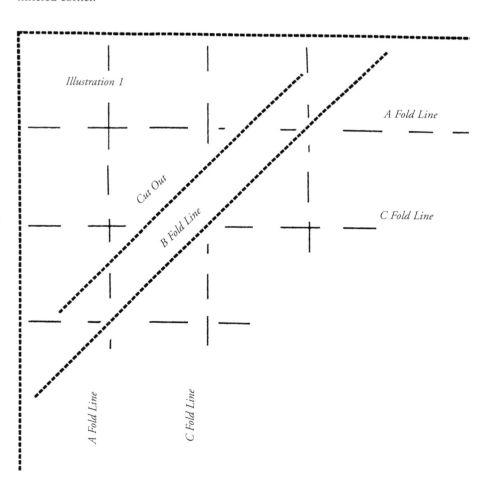

Illustration 1

Cut Out

B Fold Line

A Fold Line

A Fold Line

C Fold Line

C Fold Line

Designed by Carolyn Walker

MATERIALS

For four napkins

Cocktail Napkin Pattern on Pull-out
Four pieces white handkerchief linen,
    each $8^1/_2$" x $5^1/_2$"
Four pieces ecru batiste, each $8^1/_2$" x
    $5^1/_2$"
Floche, white and ecru
Lightweight sewing thread
#8 or #10 crewel needle and #7 between
    for embroidery
Marking pencil

CUTWORK

Trace pattern onto linen with marking pencil. Center design on grain, placing the point of design $1^3/_8$" from linen edge. Trace all parallel lines, and indicate corners at the outer edge of napkin.

With one strand of floche and a #8 crewel needle, work a small running stitch between parallel lines on the left paisley-shaped section of design. Using same thread, begin the closed buttonhole stitch with looped edge, or purl, at the outer edge of the shape (see Illustration 1A-C). Flare stitches at curves.

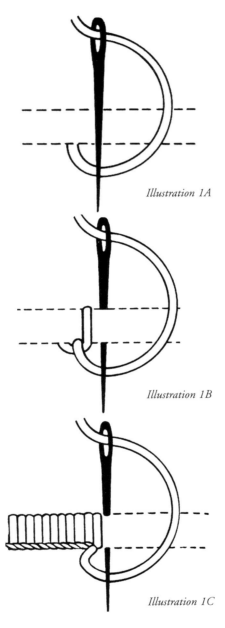

Illustration 1A

Illustration 1B

Illustration 1C

Note: Where areas are to be cut away, the purl edge must face the area to be cut.

Beginning on left side of triple arc, at the top of the design, work small running stitches. Continue around to the triple arc beneath. Upon reaching the bar lines between the two sets of arcs, carry thread across, back to starting position and back

again (three laid threads). Secure the thread each time by catching a tiny bit of fabric and the running stitch just worked. All bars should have the purl edge on the same side.

Begin working a firm, closed buttonhole over laid threads without piercing fabric. Use the eye of the needle to work bars. Continue the running stitch to second bar and work as before. Use same number of purls on each bar. Finish running stitch and begin closed buttonhole over parallel lines as before.

With one ply of ecru floss, work a small split stitch or backstitch around the small circle. This will be the support for the last bar at the bottom.

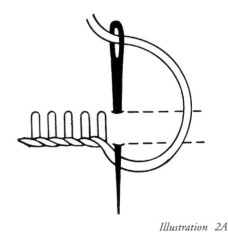

Illustration 2A

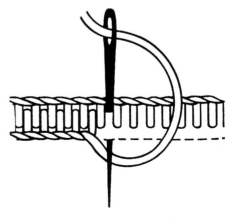

Illustration 2B

Work running stitch on double scallop portion of design base, working bar as before. Begin the double buttonhole stitch along one edge (see Illustration 2A and B).

Place stitches along other side into spaces left by first row.

Complete remaining areas. Work horizontal satin stitch over circle and point at bottom, using one strand of ecru floche or one ply floss. These two areas might also be embellished with chain stitch or outline stitch. A different stitch could be used in each napkin.

When all buttonholed areas are completed, begin cutting away areas marked with an X on design. Hold scissors parallel and close to the wrong side of the linen, with hidden scissor blade between the fabric and the purl edge. Take small snips and trim away any stray threads.

MADEIRA APPLIQUED BORDER

Place batiste over pattern and trace border design (broken line indicates seam line). Place right side of batiste to wrong side of linen and pin in place. Align point in linen design with center of border.

Working from the linen side with lightweight sewing thread and a #10 crewel needle, take small running stitches on all four sides. Reinforce corners with a couple of backstitches. Clip corner at right angles and trim seam allowance to $1/8$".

Make a cross cut in center of batiste *only* and turn batiste to right side of the linen. Turn corners out and finger press seam line.

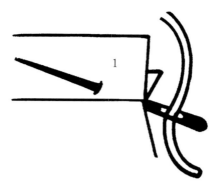

Illustration 3A

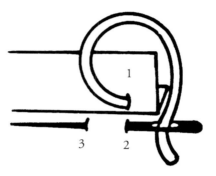

Illustration 3B

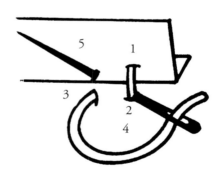

Illustration 3C

Baste $1/4$" from edge all around, placing a pin to line up centers.

Trim around design curves to within a generous $1/8$". Begin pin stitch (see Illustration 3A-C) on a short side and not in a corner. Stitch, clipping curves and turning under edge along design line.

Note: Clip inner curves to within two or three threads. Clip outer curves halfway to line. Finger press the outline an inch or so ahead of stitching.

Finger press in one direction only to achieve curves, not corners. For points, fold down top of points first, then fold under both sides. Upon reaching a corner or point with pin stitch, take two vertical stitches in same place (#1 to #2). This defines points and reinforces inner corners.

Rinse finished napkin for five minutes in cold water to remove pencil lines. Soak in very hot soapy water for five more minutes. Rinse, and press while damp, with embroidery face down on a terry towel. Trim off any remaining threads.

Designed by Roberta Chase

Note: This project uses princess lace appliqué, which is made of cotton net and cotton tapes from Belgium. Of the eight styles available, we use three: basic princess tape, small leaves and large leaves.

MATERIALS
Two 5" x 8¹/₂" pieces of cotton net
1¹/₂ yds. princess tape
4 (units) small leaves
1 (unit) large leaf

EQUIPMENT
Pattern cloth*
Fine sewing thread to match net/tapes
Basting thread (contrasting color)
#9 sharp or crewel needle
Silk dressmaker pins
Scissors
Iron & ironing board

*Construct pattern cloth by permanently transferring design onto a piece of glazed cotton chintz or other appropriate fabric. Mark grain line.

OVERVIEW
Baste cotton net into place on pattern cloth. Arrange princess tapes onto net, and baste the three layers together. With a fine sewing thread, appliqué arranged tapes to net *only*. When this is completed, remove original basting threads and the princess lace piece will separate from pattern cloth.

STEP-BY-STEP INSTRUCTIONS
Basting net onto pattern cloth: Cotton net is not very elastic, but it has less give in one direction than any other. Holes line up more clearly in this direction as well. Label this direction the grain line.

Center net over design, being sure to cover design lines on pattern cloth and line up grain line to correspond with marked pattern. With contrasting basting thread, baste along this grain line through net and grain line marked on pattern cloth.

Smooth net, being careful not to distort it in any way. Baste it to the pattern cloth around outside perimeter of jabot pattern.

Arranging tapes onto net base: Work with entire length of princess tape, cutting only when necessary. Find *pull thread* on straight edge of scalloped tape. (It will be on the very edge.) Gently push tape back on pull thread, moving gathers down tape to approximately 18 inches. These gathers will be in reserve for you as they are needed to bend around the curves of design. (If you run out of gathers at any time, find the pull thread again and gather more.)

Begin placing straight edge of tape along straight inner line of center medallion. Using gathers as necessary, gently coax tape into place, placing it flat, but smoothly, all around circle. Pin tape in place, overlapping joining by one scallop. Cut tape. (Raw edge will be on top.) With contrasting thread, baste tape through *both* net *and* pattern cloth.

Remove pins.

Place tape on each of the sides, beginning with tight rosette. Pull rosette in your hand before pinning to pattern cloth. Be sure that rosette touches medallion as indicated on pattern. Pin in place. Leave about 3 additional scallops above top of pattern design and cut tape. Baste; remove pins, as before.

With a length of princess tape, pull another tight rosette, sewing it together with matching fine sewing thread. Trim and tuck in ends. Place rosette in medallion as indicated on pattern.

Carefully separate leaves and place them as indicated. Pin, baste and remove pins. At this point press entire piece (face down).

Appliqué tapes onto net: Permanently attach lace tapes onto net with matching fine sewing thread. Beginning with a back stitch knot, whip stitch straight edge of tape onto net, with a stitch length of about ¹/₄", being careful *not* to catch pattern cloth. About every third stitch, make an additional back stitch knot.

Once all straight edges have been whipped permanently into place, make a second row of whip stitching along outer edges, just inside the scallop. At places where tapes intersect or touch each other, secure them *to each other* to strengthen piece.

When all pieces have been appliquéd to net and piece has been pressed (from the backside), remove contrasting basting stitches. Do this from the back side of the pattern cloth, keeping scissor points away from delicate net. Once removed, lace piece will easily fall away. *Carefully* clip extra net away from scalloped edges of jabot, so princess tape is now the outer edge. Do not trim excess from top of each teardrop yet.

Follow the same steps to complete second teardrop.

To assemble: Run gathering thread along top line (refer to pattern cloth) of decorated teardrop, gathering it down to size of neck of plain teardrop. Place it on top of plain teardrop, align it, and whip stitch two pieces together. To finish, wrap a length of princess tape around top raw edges and stitch together; trim net/seam allowance and enclose top edge of jabot. 🔔

"Teardrop Jabot" kit available from Roberta Chase. See Resource Guide.

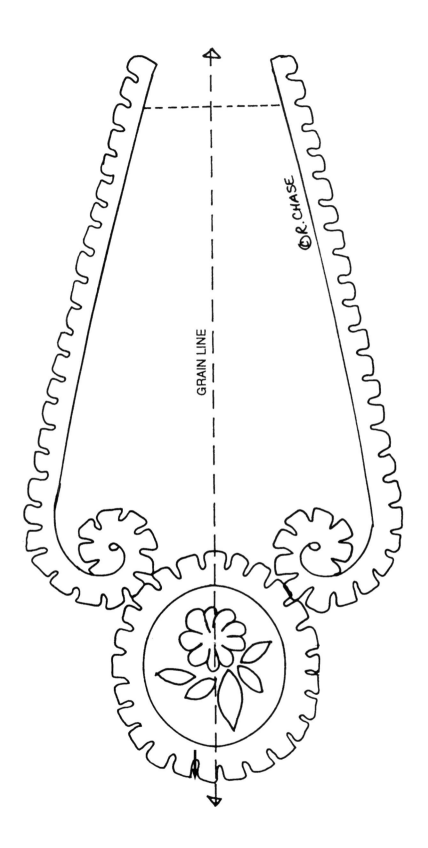

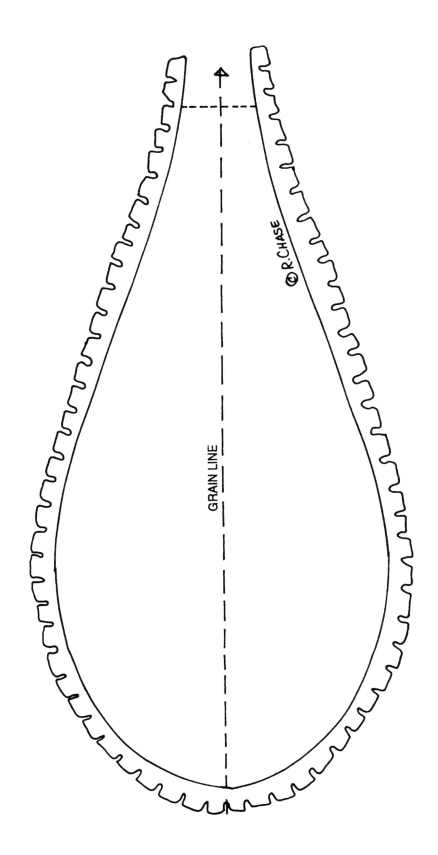

GRAIN LINE

© R.CHASE

Lace Vest *Shown on page 53*

Designed by Connie Harbor

This loose-fitting vest is designed without darts or defined waist, and is a great project to use up those valuable scraps of lace and trim.

SIZES
Small–6-8
Medium–10-12
Large–14-16
Read all directions carefully before proceeding

MATERIALS
Lace Vest Pattern on Pull-out (All sizes)
2 yds. 45" silk batiste
$^7/_8$ yd. cotton bobbinet
1 yd. 45" lightweight batting
Strips of lace insertion, edging beading, galloon sufficient to build a block for either or both vest fronts. Yardage will vary depending upon width of laces used.
Cord for piping – $4^3/_4$ yds will pipe size Large
Silk or double-faced satin ribbon, pearls, lace motifs or other embellishments
Double-faced satin ribbon for back tie, if desired

For vest and matching lining, cut three vest fronts and two vest backs from the silk, reserving a fabric piece for the fourth vest front. For a puffy look, use an underlining of a lightweight batting.

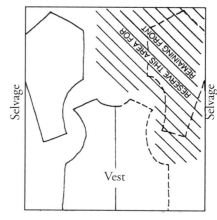

Trace vest front onto net and reserved silk; staystitch just inside drawn line with tiny zigzag stitch. Press well and re-block to shape. Do not cut these pieces out yet.

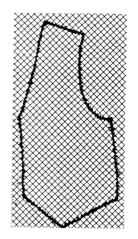

Note: After cutting, there should be
2 right fronts
1 left front
1 fabric block with left front drawn and staystitched
1 net block with left front drawn and staystitched
2 backs
1 back, two fronts from batting

Using the pattern piece as a guide, arrange lace strips side by side to create either a repeat design or asymmetrical effect. (Be creative with left-over pieces of insertion, beading, galloon and edgings.)

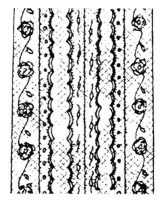

Using a narrow, moderate length zigzag stitch, join the lace strips side by side to form a block to fit the vest front. Press well after each piece is joined.

Lightly spray net with sizing.

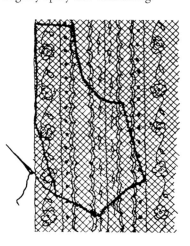

Immediately place lace block over staystitched shape and lightly respray with sizing. Press well. (The sizing will help bond the two layers to prevent shifting.) Pin lace block in place over net. Hand baste along staystitched line and repress.

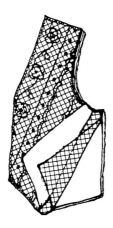

Layer lace/net block over fabric reserved for the fourth vest front and hand baste along staystitched line. Press, then machine stitch along hand-basted line. Press well. Cut vest front just outside staystitched line and treat this layered block as one piece of fabric for remainder of construction.

Baste batting underlining to vest fronts and back. Sew vest fronts to vest back at shoulders. Trim bulk from seam allowance. Sew lining fronts to lining back at shoulders. Press seams open. Staystitch lining on side seam lines and press seam allowance to wrong side, setting crease well. Set lining aside.

Measure outside edges of vest to determine yardage needed for piping. Cut and join bias strips to this measurement.

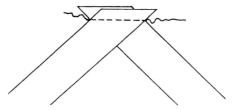

Sew piping across bottom of vest back, around armholes, and from vest side front, around neck to vest side front, clipping into piping seam allowance to turn points and corners. Press.

Note: A grooved clear appliqué foot holds the piping in place and simplifies turning points and corners.

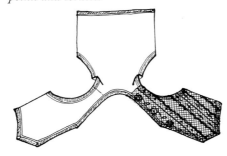

Pin lining to corded vest, right sides together. If batting underlining was used, hand basting is recommended before sewing vest to lining on the corded piping seam line.

Note: A grooved foot will ride over corded piping and simplify this stitching technique. Stitch around vest, leaving sides open. Press well. Trim seam and overcast or serge. Clip at points and corners. Turn right side out through side opening.

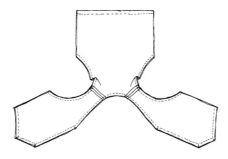

Press edges on right side and carefully stitch in the ditch around the corded piping. This stitching should be virtually invisible; it replaces the need for understitching and creates a knife edge.

Note: An edge stitch foot (with a center blade to guide the needle) simplifies this stitching technique.

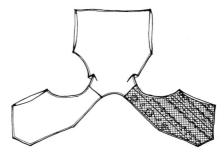

At side openings, pin right sides together and stitch, beginning about 2" beyond the underarm and ending about 2" beyond the hem. Carefully press this seam open, using the point of iron.

Lining seam allowances will fall to the inside on the crease line. Opening can be neatly and easily slipstitched closed.

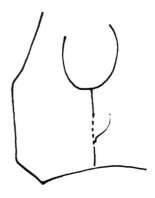

Embellishment: A welt pocket may be made from lace scraps or any other lace, ribbon or trim embellishment may be added. Create a personal fashion statement with a gathered lace edge flounce, ribbon rosette or lace hanky peeking from a silk pocket with ribbon binding. ❧

Stationery Folio *Shown on pages 54 & 55*

Designed by Janelle Cox

MATERIALS

Stationery Folio pattern on Pull-out
Fabric used for case is cotton/linen blend
2 pieces of pink fabric, 11^1/$_2$" x 17"
   (One piece is for the front cover and
   one for inside lining. Seam
   allowances are ^{1}/$_2$"; finished size is
   10^1/$_2$" x 16".)
2 pieces pink fabric 7" x 11^1/$_2$" for inside
   pockets (finished size of pocket is 5" by
   10^1/$_2$")
2 pieces grey fabric 2" x 11^1/$_2$" for
   teardrop appliqués on inside pockets
1 piece grey fabric 3^1/$_2$" x 5^1/$_2$" for
   teardrop appliqué on front
Small pieces of pink and grey fabric for
   flower appliqués
Pellon® fleece 11^1/$_2$" x 17"
1 yd. ^{1}/$_4$" pink ribbon for ties
1 yd. ^{1}/$_8$" grey ribbon for ties
12" square pink Swiss batiste for
   handkerchief (finished size 9" square)
Fine sewing thread to match batiste
Needles: #26 tapestry for shadow stitch
   and pinstitching; #7 between for
   buttonhole; #12 sharp for all other
   embroidery
Water soluble marker

COLOR KEY

#1–762 grey floche
#2–744 yellow floche
#3–369 green floche
#4–3689 pink floche
#5–flesh floche
#6–DMC 369 green
#7–DMC 744 yellow
#8–DMC 762 grey
#9–DMC 834 gold
#10–DMC 963 pink
#11–DMC 3042 purple

STITCH KEY

A–Granitos   F–Buttonhole
B–Outline stitch   G–Pin stitch
C–French knots   H–Double-sided
D–Backstitch   buttonhole
E–Satin stitch   I–Shadow stitch

INSTRUCTIONS

1. Transfer all embroidery designs onto fabric with water soluble marker. Match grainlines of main fabric piece (hereafter referred to as MFP) and appliqué pieces.

2. Baste 3^1/$_2$" x 5^1/$_2$" grey appliqué piece to front cover of MFP.

3. Pad teardrop shapes with a double strand of grey floche, then buttonhole with single strand of grey floche, stitching through both fabric pieces. Trim away grey fabric along purled edges.

4. Pad letters of monogram with backstitch. Satin stitch over padding using grey floche. After satin stitching first initial, backstitch as indicated with DMC 3042 for added emphasis. Then work remaining embroidery using floche for flowers and DMC for other details. Note: For monograms, refer to *Victorian Alphabets, Monograms and Names for Needleworkers,* and *Old Fashioned Monogramming for Needleworkers,* both from Dover. Another source for alphabets is a favorite font from your home computer.

5. Baste 2" x 11^1/$_2$" strip of grey teardrop shapes to inner edges of both pocket pieces. Pad and buttonhole with grey floche, stitching through both pieces. Leave open those areas indicated for flower petals to extend into pocket edges to be stitched later.

6. Backstitch veins of leaves with grey floche. Baste leaves to MFP, pad and buttonhole through both pieces. Trim leaf fabric from purled edges.

7. Baste stem to MFP along one side of stem. Turn in ^{1}/$_8$" and pinstitch opposite side from basting with grey floche, covering unfinished leaf edge. Remove basting; turn under ^{1}/$_8$" and pinstitch along other side.

Note: Unfinished edges of appliqué that are covered by an adjoining piece do not need to be turned in ^{1}/$_8$".

8. Turning in ^{1}/$_8$" and using grey floche, baste and pinstitch base of flower to MFP, covering stem edge.

9. Backstitch details in all flower petals with pink floche.

10. Turning in ^{1}/$_8$", baste and pinstitch two side petals to main flower appliqué with DMC 963.

11. Buttonhole stitch front appliqué petal with grey floche and trim fabric from purled edge.

12. Fold under ^{1}/$_8$" on remaining edge of front petal. Baste and pinstitch with DMC 963 to MFP.

13. French knot center of flower.

14. Turning in ^{1}/$_8$" and using grey floche, baste and pinstitch appliqué flower to MFP at lower edge.

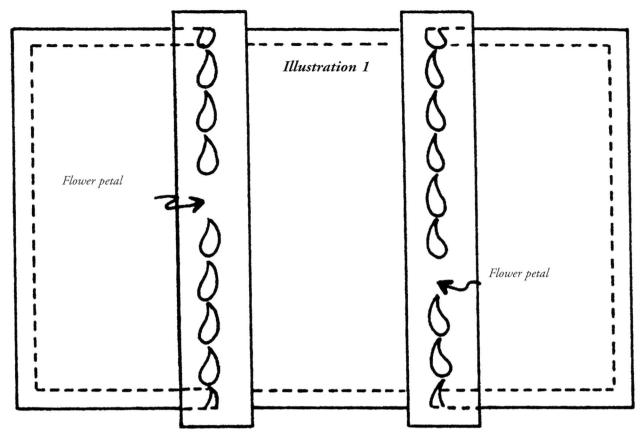

Flower petal

Illustration 1

Flower petal

15. Buttonhole stitch around the two side petals to MFP, stitching through both fabric layers to the Xs indicated on left pocket and right pocket pattern pieces. At Xs, continue buttonhole stitching around top of flower only on appliqué piece. Do not stitch through both fabric pieces. This leaves an opening at the top of flower for a pocket. Trim appliqué flower along purls. ·

16. Trim MFP and appliqué flower petal along purls of outer edge of pocket.

17. Complete remainder of embroidery stitches as indicated on left and right pocket pieces.

18. Repeat for other pocket.

19. Wash thoroughly and iron face down on towel. Spray starch.

CONSTRUCTION OF CASE
1. Baste fleece to wrong side of monogrammed front piece. Trim fleece $1/4$".

2. Baste wrong side of pockets to right

side of inside lining.

3. Pin monogrammed piece and inside lining together, right sides together.

4. Cut ribbons in half and tack ribbons at side seams for ties.

5. Stitch in $1/2$" seam, leaving an opening at the bottom for turning. Trim seams and clip corners diagonally.

6. Turn to right side and press. Press in seam allowance of opening.

7. Slip stitch opening closed.

HANDKERCHIEF
1. Transfer design with water soluble marker.

2. Pad and satin stitch monogram with DMC 762, then backstitch with DMC 3042.

3. Shadow stitch teardrops with grey floche.

4. Work remaining embroidery stitches.

5. Pad lower edge for cutwork with a doubled strand of DMC 762 and work double-sided buttonhole stitch over padding with #12 sharp needle and one strand. This cutwork edge is also worked on the opposite corner of handkerchief.

6. Trim away fabric at cutwork edge, being careful to trim so that the appliqué hem can be turned up and cut ends can be slip stitched at cutwork edge. Trim fabric inside teardrop shapes.

7. Fold hem on fold line, finger press and baste close to fold. Miter corners. Fold under $1/8$" of raw edge; clip as necessary. Finger press and baste. Pinstitch hem with fine sewing thread.

8. Wash thoroughly and iron face down. Spray starch. &

Designed by Carol Clements

MATERIALS

Doll clothing patterns on Pull-out
Knickers or jumper: $1/2$ yd. 45" fabric
Blouse or shirt: $3/8$ yd. 45" fabric
Piping: $3/8$ - $1/2$ yd.
Scrap of fabric for bib lining

Notions: Thread, mini-piping cord, 4/0
snaps. $1/8$" buttons (2 for knickers, 5 for
blouse or shirt)

*Note: The photographed garments feature
machine embroidered motifs from a
programmed design card. Gingerbread
figures may also be hand embroidered,
appliquéd, or even painted on the fabric.
Gingerbread shape for appliqué is included
on Pattern Pull-out.*

For embroidery, cut a piece of fabric large
enough to fit in machine embroidery
frame. Embroider design using rayon or
desired embroidery thread. Remove
finished design from frame and cut bib,
centering design on pattern piece.

INSTRUCTIONS

*Note: Read all instructions before
beginning. All seam allowances are $1/4$"
unless otherwise indicated. Please note that
drawings are not necessarily to scale.*

The forest green poplin and white
Imperial broadcloth are somewhat heavier
than fabrics often used for doll clothes
and require a special seam finish. Seams
are first stitched normally, with right

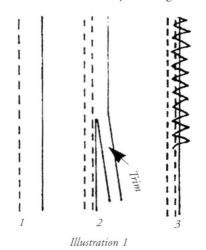

Illustration 1

sides together, using a $1/4$" seam
allowance. Stitch seam again $1/8$" away
from first stitching. Trim away excess
fabric. Set machine for zigzag stitch,
(length 1, width $3^{1}/2$). Zigzag off edge of
seam for a neatly finished seam.

BLOUSE OR SHIRT

Blouse: Fold right front facing to outside
(right side) of right blouse front.

Fold left front facing to inside or wrong
side of left blouse front. Press both
facings into place.

On right front, topstitch close to both
folds as illustrated.

On left front, edgestitch only one side.
Press.

Shirt: Reverse the above process and fold
left front to outside of left shirt front;
fold right front facing to inside. Proceed
as for blouse, topstitching close to both
folds on left front; edgestitch on right
front.

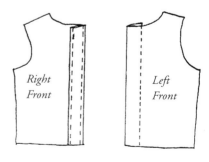

Illustration 2

French seam blouse front to blouse back
at shoulder seams.

*Note: For fabrics with a definite right and
wrong side, press both facings to wrong side.*

COLLAR

Baste piping to collar. Pin collar pieces,
with right sides together, and stitch,

leaving neck edge open. Trim seam to scant $\frac{1}{8}$". Turn collar right side out and press. Baste raw edges of neck together.

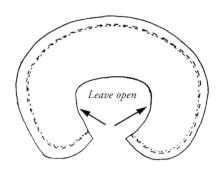

Illustration 3

Matching center fronts and center backs, pin collar to neck edge. Baste.

Cut a bias strip 1" wide by approximately 8" long. Fold bias strip in half lengthwise and press carefully, taking care not to stretch bias. Pin bias strip to neck edge, matching raw edges. Trim excess length allowing $\frac{1}{4}$" at each front edge to fold under. Baste. Stitch as illustrated.

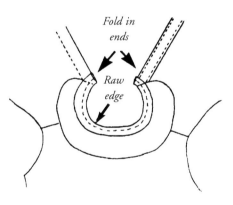

Illustration 4

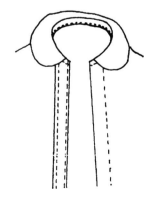

Illustration 5

Trim seam, clip if necessary. Fold bias to inside of blouse or shirt. Press. Edgestitch folded edge of bias into place.

SLEEVES
Fold sleeve placket extensions in as illustrated. Press and edgestitch into place.

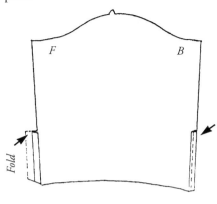

Illustration 6

Sew a row of lengthened machine stitching along sleeve cap just inside seam line.

For blouse, run two rows of lengthened machine stitching along sleeve cap and at wrist edge.

For shirt, mark pleats at cuff edge with tiny clips. Fold pleats along arrows on pattern piece. Pin and press pleats. Baste. Sew one row of lengthened machine stitching along sleeve cap just inside seam line.

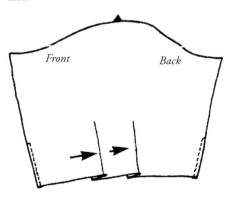

Illustration 7

CUFFS
Press under $\frac{1}{4}$" along two (of four) cuff pieces. Trim pressed seam slightly.

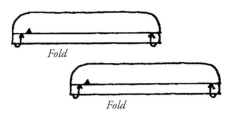

Illustration 8

Baste piping to remaining cuff pieces.

With right sides together, stitch one cuff to each remaining cuff piece. Trim seam. Turn cuffs right side out. Press.

Illustration 9

Pin cuff to wrist edge of sleeve with right sides together. For blouse, pull up gathers and adjust evenly to fit. For shirt, stitch and trim seam. Press seam toward cuff; press cuff over seam, encasing it. Slipstitch cuff into place by hand.

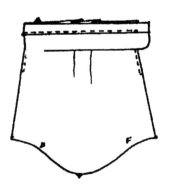

Illustration 10

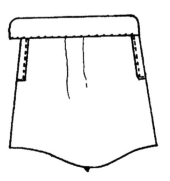

Illustration 11

SETTING IN SLEEVES

With right sides together, pin sleeves to blouse or shirt, matching notch to shoulder seam. For blouse, pull up gathers and adjust evenly to fit. For shirt, use gathering thread to adjust ease.

Stitch sleeves to blouse or shirt; finish seam. With right sides together, pin side seams and sleeve seams. Stitch, tapering at sleeve opening as illustrated. Finish seam.

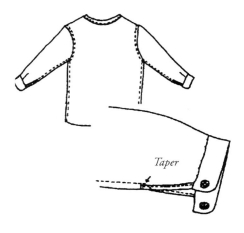

Taper

Illustrations 12 and 13

HEM

Press under ¹/₄" along raw edge; press under another ¹/₄". Edgestitch hem into place.

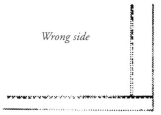

Wrong side

Illustration 14

FINISHING

Sew snaps and buttons at Xs as indicated on pattern piece. Girl's blouse front laps right over left; boy's shirt laps left over right. Sew snaps to cuffs as illustrated.

BIB JUMPER OR KNICKERS

Bib (both views): Baste and sew piping to upper edge of bib. Stitch upper bib band to bib.

On opposite side of band, stitch bib lining. Press bib lining to wrong side of bib as illustrated, having raw edges even. Baste raw edges together.

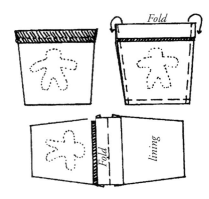

Fold

Fold   *lining*

Illustration 15

STRAPS

Pin right side of strap to wrong side of bib. Stitch as illustrated. Press seam allowance toward strip; press in remainder of strap seam allowance. Press seam allowance along other side of strap.

Fold strap around to bib front, encasing seam allowance. Press. Edgestitch strap into place, folding in ends, as illustrated.

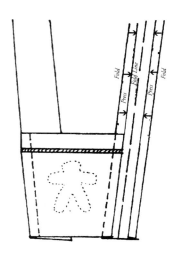

Illustration 16

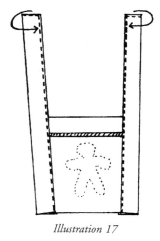

Illustration 17

Mark pleats on either skirt or knickers front with tiny clips. Fold pleats along lines in direction of arrows. Pin baste and press.

For knickers, with right sides together, sew center front and center back seams. Finish seams. Press.

For skirt or knickers back casing, fold under ¹/₄" along upper edge and press. Turn under and press an additional ¹/₂". Edgestitch casing into place.

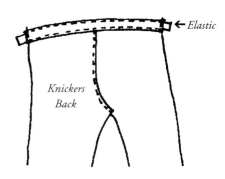

← *Elastic*

Knickers Back

Illustration 18

For both views, insert a 6" piece of ³/₈" elastic in casing, extending each end of elastic ¹/₂" beyond casing. Pin. Machine baste to hold elastic in place.

WAISTBAND

Baste and stitch piping to upper edge of one waistband piece.

With right sides together, pin other long side of waistband to knickers or skirt front, carefully matching center fronts. Stitch. Press seam toward waistband. Edgestitch.

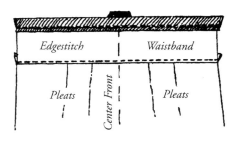

Edgestitch   *Waistband*

Pleats   *Center Front*   *Pleats*

Illustration 19

Pin finished bib to piped edge of waistband, right sides together, matching center fronts. Pin and baste. Stitch bib into place.

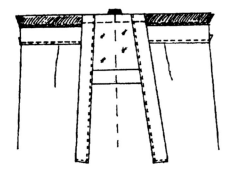

Illustration 20

Press under ¼" along remaining waistband piece (to be used as a facing).

With right sides together, pin waistband facing to waistband. Stitch. Press seam toward waistband.

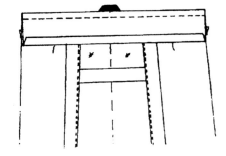

Illustration 21

For jumper, with right sides together, pin skirt back to front at side seams. Top of back casing should be even with top seamline in front waistband. Stitch side seams, trim and zigzag to finish. Press seams toward skirt front. Turn waistband to inside of skirt, enclosing back casing ends and seam. Slipstitch waistband over seam and casing.

For knickers, stitch front to back at inner leg or crotch seam. Stitch; finish seam and press toward back.

LEGBANDS
Fold in extensions along lower leg and stitch, as illustrated.

Run two rows of lengthened machine stitches along lower edge of knickers.

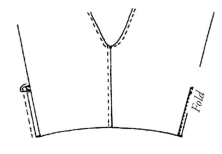

Illustration 22

With right sides together, pin knickers to legbands, as illustrated, placing back extension along extension line. Pull up gathers and adjust evenly to fit. Stitch legband. Press seam toward legband. Repeat for other side.

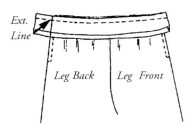

Illustration 23

With right sides together, fold legbands, lengthwise, along foldline. Stitch ends, trim seams and fold legband to inside of pants, encasing raw edges. Press. Slipstitch legband into place.

With right sides together, pin knickers fronts to back at side seams. Top of back casing should be even with seamline of waistband. Stitch side seams, tapering at leg extensions. Finish seam; press toward fronts. Slipstitch waistband into place as described for jumper.

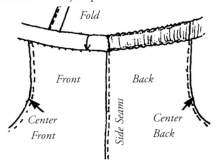

Illustration 24

FINISHING
For both views, measure one inch over from center back and mark with pin. Sew snap, centered on casing, at this point. Sew other portion of snap at end of strap. Adjust placement if necessary.

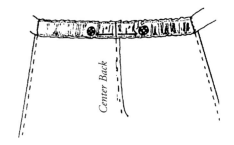

Illustration 25

For jumper, turn under ¼" along lower edge; press. Edgestitch. Turn up hem additional 1⅛". Press. Slipstitch hem into place.

Sew snaps and buttons on legbands for knickers as indicated by Xs on pattern piece. &

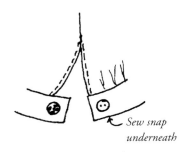

Sew snap underneath

Illustration 26

Designed by Sharon Sparks Newton

MATERIALS
Pattern and design on Pattern Pull-out
1 yd. 60" green fabric for apron
Scraps of white, red, green, black and
light blue for appliqué pieces *(Note: Christmas prints and mini dots work well)*
Wonder Under™ by Pellon for appliqué
pieces
Red pompom for nose
Two 1" sew-on movable eyes
1 small red button for holly berry
2 metal or plastic D rings for buckle

INSTRUCTIONS
Apron
Cut out main apron piece. Finish all edges by pressing under $1/4$". Fold under another $1/4$"; press. Top stitch completely around apron.

Pocket
Cut a rectangle $10^3/4$" x $17^1/2$" for pocket. Across top, press under $1/4$", then fold under another $1/4$" and top stitch. Repeat for sides and lower edge of pocket. Stitch to apron. The pocket should be centered and the lower edge should be about $6^1/2$" from finished lower edge of apron. Sew from center top of pocket to center bottom to divide pocket into two.

Side Ties
Cut two strips of fabric $2^1/2$" x 24". Fold under and press $1/4$" down on all sides. Fold in half and top stitch around. Finished width of ties will be 1". Stitch to apron sides.

Neck Strap and Buckle
Cut one strip of fabric $2^1/2$" x $22^1/2$". Finish in a similar manner to side ties. Stitch to left side of apron top.

Cut one strip of fabric $2^1/2$" x 3". Finish as before. Loop around D rings and stitch to right side of apron top.

Appliqué
Fuse all appliqué fabric with Wonder Under™, following manufacturer's directions. Trace appliqué pattern on paper side. Cut out.

Iron appliqué on apron and stitch, using a close zigzag or satin stitch around appliqué edges. Stitch background pieces first. Layer appliqués in following order: (1) face and hands; (2) top of hat and hatband; (3) hat brim; (4) main bow piece; (5) bow knot; (6) mouth, pipe and smoke; (7) holly leaves.

Finish by adding eyes, nose and button for holly berry. ❧

Designed by Carolyn Walker

MATERIALS
Dove Bib Pattern on Pull-out
Linen or Ramie, 17" x 13" for bib
Batiste, 4" x 4" for appliqués
36" length of $^3/_8$" white ribbon
One small button
Floche
    Blanc Neige (white)
    666 Red
    700 Green
    640 Brown
    334 Blue
    444 Yellow
#7 between needle
Water soluble marker or graphite pencil

ORDER OF WORK
Transfer designs to base fabric and appliqué fabric. A light mist of hair spray will prevent the design from smudging as work progresses.

1. Stitch pieces to be appliquéd first. Work a small closed blanket/buttonhole stitch around detached wing (3) and tail (2) using white floche. Stitch ribbon around dove's neck in shadow work, using red floche.

2. Cut out back wing (1) and pinstitch onto bib, clipping curves as needed. (Fine sewing thread may be used for pinstitch.) The area to be covered with the bird's head may be left loose or basted in place.

3. With right side up, carefully trim away excess fabric from embroidered tail and wing portions. Cut out remainder of body (2) and wing (3) along dashed selvage lines.

4. Pinstitch the body in place, using fine thread; overlap head onto wing (1). Do not attach tail portion which was buttonhole-stitched; this area is left open.

5. With white floche, pinstitch remaining wing (3) onto body along dashed line only. Pull stitches tightly to make wing cup. Stitch through all layers of fabric.

6. With yellow floche, satin stitch beak. With brown floche, stem stitch holly branch.

7. Using center vein as a guideline, work holly leaves in green. Stitch one-half of the leaf in satin stitch; define remaining area in stem stitch. Reverse placement of stitches on remaining leaf.

8. The three berries are red floche granitos.* Dove's eye is a blue granito, worked through all layers of fabric. Streamers are a continuation of collar, stitched in red shadow work.

9. The design beneath dove is worked entirely in white floche. Petals are padded satin stitch, circles are granitos, and lines are stem stitch.

10. Stitch scallops around bib in closed blanket/buttonhole stitch. Begin at lower right side and, including straight edge of ribbon casing, work around to beginning of neck area. Repeat for other side, beginning at neck.

11. Run basting threads along dashed casing line and around solid line of neck edge. Soak *uncut* bib in warm soapy water, until tracing lines are no longer visible. Rinse well and iron face down in a terry towel while bib is still fairly damp. Trim excess fabric from scallops *only;* leave neck opening intact.

12. Finger-press hem edge under $^1/_8$"; place folded edge along previously basted line and pinstitch in place with fine thread to form casing.

13. With right sides together, stitch bias strip to neck edge with tiny running stitches, using basting stitches as guidelines. Cut out neck opening, leaving a generous $^1/_8$" allowance. Turn bias strip to back, fold in raw edges at back neck opening and turn under long raw edge $^1/_8$". Slip stitch loose edge in place to meet running stitches.

14. Sew small button onto right neck edge of bib. Make a chained or buttonholed loop on left side to fit button. Run ribbon through casing (this will be snug) and notch ends of ribbon. Knot each end of ribbon above notched ends.

* A granito is a small, satin "bump" stitch formed by making several small stitches on top of each other. Six or seven stitches produce a small granito; ten to twelve a larger one (as in the eye of the dove). It is most easily worked with needle emerging at bottom of design area and sinking to back at top. 🪡

Designed by Carolyn Walker

MATERIALS

One 8" x 8" square of batiste
One 2¹/₂" x 16" strip of batiste
20" lace insertion
1³/₄ yd. lace edging
40" Swiss beading with entredeux edge
16" entredeux
1¹/₂ yds ¹/₄" wide ribbon
8" x 18" fleece (for padding)
#8 or #10 crewel needle
Oval 5" x 7" basket
Tacky® glue
Beeswax
Water soluble pen
3" x 8" paper puffing guide

1. Pull a strip of fabric on grain 3" wide by 8" long (down selvage edge). Measure ¹/₂" from right lengthwise side; pull a single thread slightly to crimp fabric. *Do not remove thread.* Finger press along crimped line.

2. Make a pin tuck along fold using tiny running stitches. Measure ¹/₄" over from first pin tuck toward center of fabric and make another tuck.

3. Roll and whip edge of fabric nearest the first pin tuck.

4. Trim batiste from one side of Swiss beading. Pin beading to rolled edge of batiste with right sides together, and batiste on top. Insert needle under roll and up through hole of entredeux edge; whip together going into each hole. Turn and press.

5. Trim remaining side of beading; with right sides together, whip to an 8" strip of lace insertion.

6. Crease brown paper strip in half; finger press long batiste strip in half and pin to paper at ends and center. (Strip for puffing is always twice the finished length.) Lightly wax thread. Rolling and whipping as before, pull thread to gather up roll every 7 to 10 stitches. Upon reaching center pin, even out gathers to lie flat against paper; take two stitches over roll in same hole to secure thread, and proceed as before to the end of strip. Work other side of strip in same manner. Even out gathers to lie opposite each other. *Do not remove from paper!*

7. Cut away batiste from an 8" strip of entredeux and pin face down on paper next to one rolled edge, and whip together. Repeat on other side of puffing strip; then remove from paper.

8. Clip away remaining batiste from entredeux and whip to the unstitched edge of insertion lace on tucked panel.

9. Make another tucked panel, mirror image, attaching Swiss beading and insertion lace as before. Be sure that patterns in lace and holes line up with those in first panel *(see Illustration 1)*.

10. Cut three layers of padding, using top of basket as a pattern. Trim away ¹/₂" from one layer, 1" from another. Stack and glue the three layers, smallest first, then medium, then large, to basket cover. Glue around edge of top layer and press in place.

11. Run ribbon through beading in completed batiste top. Pin around top edge of basket lid. Make sure that batiste is smooth and on grain. Mark oval edge with water soluble marker; remove from basket and stay-stitch marked oval (machine or handstitch). Trim to within ³/₄" of staystitching and pin again to basket lid as before. Run a thin line of glue around side of basket top, gluing a small section at a time and pressing down edge of batiste as glue is applied. Trim away excess fabric *(see Illustration 2 and 3)*.

12. Cut Swiss beading to fit snugly around side of basket top, add ¹/₂" to measurement. Overlap edges ¹/₄" each end; folding top edge under slightly, whip together *(see Illustration 4)*.

13. Cut lace edging in half. Pull a heavy thread in the heading of one section to gather. Adjust gathered lace evenly to fit Swiss beading and, right sides together, whip lace to entredeux edge of beading. overlap raw ends of lace, turn under top edge and whip or blanket stitch together. Repeat on other side of beading.

14. Thread ribbon through beading and slip ruffled band over padded basket lid. Using a toothpick and glue, apply dots of glue every inch along basket side, pulling away band from sides of the basket at the bottom. Press band into place *(see Illustration 5)*. 🍂

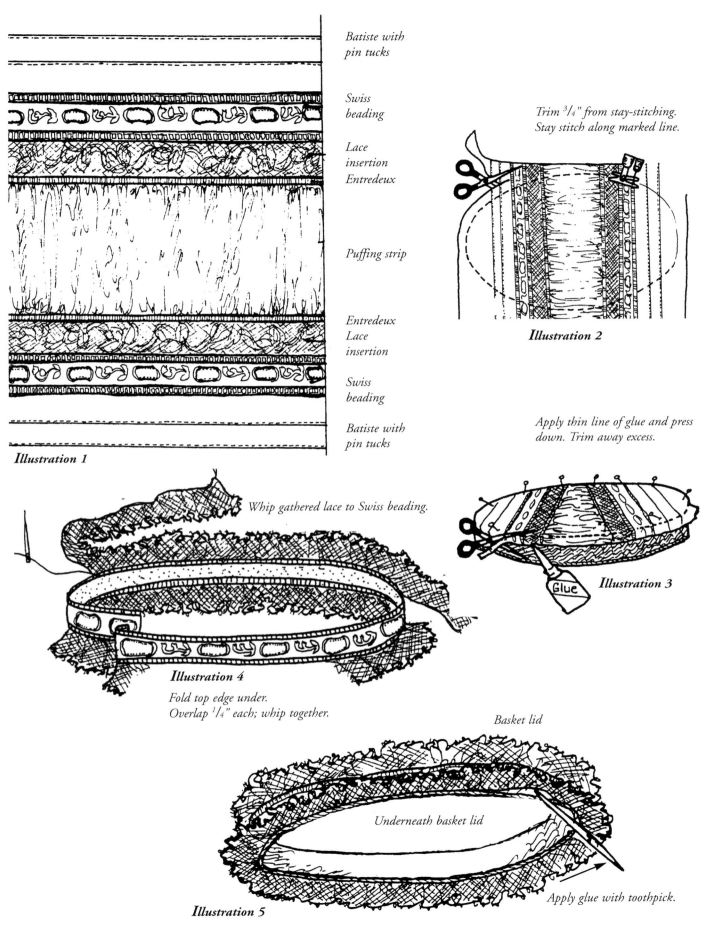

Batiste with
pin tucks

Swiss
beading

Lace
insertion
Entredeux

Puffing strip

Entredeux
Lace
insertion

Swiss
beading

Batiste with
pin tucks

Illustration 1

Trim ³/₄" from stay-stitching.
Stay stitch along marked line.

Illustration 2

Apply thin line of glue and press
down. Trim away excess.

Whip gathered lace to Swiss beading.

Illustration 3

Glue

Illustration 4

Fold top edge under.
Overlap ¹/₄" each; whip together.

Basket lid

Underneath basket lid

Apply glue with toothpick.

Illustration 5

A Creative Needle Christmas 153

Designed by Nancy Newell

CHOCOLATE A

1. Cut three pieces of $^5/_8$" (or $^7/_8$") wide ribbon, each $4^1/_2$" (or $6^1/_2$") long.

2. With right sides together, whip two pieces of ribbon together along one long edge. (Option: Sew by machine. With right sides together, zigzag over edge of ribbon, just catching selvages of both pieces. Set stitch length to about 15-20 stitches per inch. Stitches will zigzag off side of ribbon, so stitch width is variable.) Add the third piece of ribbon to long edge of one side of ribbon strip. Three pieces are now sewn together.

3. Fold ribbon piece in half, right sides together, to form a tube. Seam across cut ends, using a $^1/_4$" seam allowance.

4. Using double thread, sew running stitches along each edge of tube and pull

tightly to gather. Before pulling up second side, add a small amount of polyester fiberfil to stuff.

5. Optional: Tack on ribbon rose.

CHOCOLATE B

1. Cut one piece of $^5/_8$" (or $^7/_8$") wide double-faced satin ribbon to a 30"-36" length.

2. With fabric marking pen, mark every $^3/_4$" (or one inch) along ribbon.

3. Fold ribbon at each mark to form a zigzag. Sew through each fold along one edge of ribbon and pull up tightly to form circle.

4. Finish ribbon ends by overcasting together at bottom of chocolate.

CHOCOLATE C

1. Cut two pieces of ribbon each 2" or 3" long. On both ends of each piece, fold under $^1/_2$" seam allowance and fingerpress. These two pieces will be top the top and bottom of petit fours.

2. Cut another piece of ribbon 5" (or 7") long for side piece. With right sides together, whip side piece to top piece. Begin at one corner of top and leave a $^1/_2$" seam allowance on side piece; turn at corners and sew side piece to folded edge. Repeat for bottom piece.

3. Stuff through corner opening of side piece, using a small amount of polyester fiberfil. Slip stitch opening closed.

4. Decorate top with ribbon rose or

zigzag ribbon trim.

Zigzag ribbon trim: Use $^1/_4$" or $^3/_8$" wide satin ribbon. Sew running stitches on a zigzag path down ribbon and gather up as much ribbon as is desired for trim. Zigzag path can be marked with a fabric marking pen, marking about $^3/_4$" apart along one edge, or gathering can be stitched by "eye."

CHOCOLATE D

The fourth variation is very similar to Chocolate C, except the ribbon sides are puffed or gathered. Cut a piece of ribbon for sides approximately 10" (or 14") long and whip over each edge, pulling up to gather to approximately 5" (or 7") long. Use this gathered piece to complete the chocolates or petit fours as in Chocolate C. Tack on ribbon rose. 🍃

"Ribbon Chocolates" kit available from Gardner's Ribbons and Lace. See Resource Guide.

Designed by Tina Lewis

Any gardener would appreciate a handsome set of hand tools and gardening gloves in this canvas storage bag with a generous pocket for seeds. Decorative hand stitching and embroidery can be replaced with machine stitchery if time is of the essence.

SUPPLIES

$^1/_3$ yd. heavyweight natural canvas
Scraps of Ultrasuede® in four earthtone colors (red, rust, green and brown are suggestions)
DMC embroidery floss: black 310
One 72" leather shoelace

Cut a 9" x 27" piece of canvas for bag. Cut a 6" x 9" piece of canvas for pocket. Cut a 4" x 6" piece of red suede for appliqué. Cut two pieces of red suede $2^1/_2$" x 10" for casings.

Trace three designs (sprout, sky and earth) from appliqué diagram. Follow dotted underlap lines for sky and sprout pieces. Cut sprout of green suede, sky of rust and earth of brown.

Transfer the word "Cultivate" to the canvas bag piece centered from side to

Gardener's Bag

side and on a line 12" down from the top of the bag. Using 3 strands of floss, embroider "Cultivate" in backstitch.

For pocket, turn under side and bottom edges of pocket $^1/_2$" and press. Turn top edge under $^1/_4$" and again 1" to form hem. Hand or machine stitch hem.

Assemble appliqué by placing sprout on sky following diagram. Using a leather needle and 3 strands of black floss, appliqué with a small running stitch close to edges and in center of leaves as indicated. All decorative stitching can also be done by machine. Lap earth piece $1/4$" over sky and edgestitch in place.

Pink edges of appliqué. Place finished appliqué on 4"x 6" piece of red suede and stitch all around, $1/4$" from pinked edge. Pink edges of red piece. Center entire piece on pocket and stitch $1/4$" from pinked edge all around.

Set finished pocket on bag, centering side to side with the bottom edge of the pocket touching the top of the embroidered letters. Edgestitch pocket in place along sides and base.

Fold bag in half and pin side seams, right sides together. Stitch sides in $1/2$" seams. Finish edges by serging or zigzagging. To box corners, fold bottom corners of the bag into triangles by bringing side seams in line with base of bag. Stitch across corners 1" from points. Turn bag right side out.

Fold ends of each casing piece in 1" and press. Pink long edges of both casing pieces. Fold casings in half lengthwise, wrong sides together, and press. Enclose top edge of front of bag with one casing piece. Stitch casing to bag through all three layers, $1/4$" from pinked edges. Repeat for back casing piece. Whip together folded ends of casings on the inside of the bag, leaving outside of casing open to accommodate drawstring.

Cut shoelace in half. Thread one piece through one side of the casing, around and out the same opening. Thread other piece of shoelace through the other side of casing, around and out the same opening. Knot shoelaces together on each side. 🍂

The Cook's Bag *Shown on page 62*

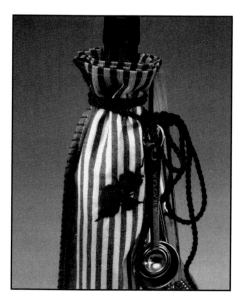

Designed by Tina Lewis

A tall bottle of raspberry vinegar inside an embroidered dish towel bag tied with measuring spoons, a whisk and salad tongs makes an ideal gift for any cook. The bag is not cut during construction so that when the large whip stitches on the sides of the bag are snipped, the towel itself becomes part of the gift. Machine embroidered designs could also be used. For different sized bottles, experiment with alternative folding methods.

This bag is sized for a $14^{1}/_{4}$" x $2^{1}/_{2}$" bottle.
SUPPLIES
One $21^{1}/_{2}$" x $29^{1}/_{2}$" dish towel
DMC embroidery floss 890, 816, 814
$1^{3}/_{4}$ yds. purchased cording

Press dish towel. Center embroidery design in upper left corner of towel, $4^{1}/_{2}$" from top and $2^{3}/_{4}$" from side.

To embroider the raspberries, transfer design to towel. Using a small hoop, work leaves in satin stitch, stems in stem stitch

Cook's Bag

using 3 strands DMC 890. Raspberries are worked in French knots, using 6 strands DMC 816 or 814 stitched at random. 🍂

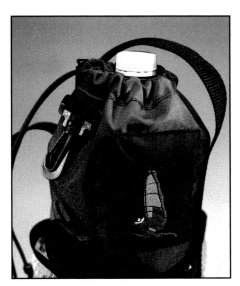

Designed by Tina Lewis

Treat an active teen to a carrier for a tall bottle of water or thirst quencher. Bag has four mesh pockets for essential gear, a carrying strap and a tiny machine embroidered money pocket.

This bag is sized for 12$^{1}/_{2}$" x 3$^{1}/_{4}$" bottle.

SUPPLIES

$^{1}/_{2}$ yd. green sports nylon for bag
$^{1}/_{4}$ yd. mesh for pockets
$^{3}/_{4}$ yd. black fold-over binding
60 inches 1" nylon strapping
Two "D" rings
One swivel strap hook
One $^{1}/_{2}$" Velcro® dot
Scraps of purple sports nylon for pocket
1 yd. $^{1}/_{8}$" nylon or elastic cording
One double cord lock

Cut one 16" x 28" piece of green nylon for the bag. Cut a 20" x 7" piece of mesh for the pockets. Cut two 5$^{7}/_{8}$" circles of green nylon ($^{1}/_{2}$" seam allowances included) and baste together as one. Mark half points at either side. Cut two pocket flaps of purple nylon.

Trace pocket piece on purple nylon and, before cutting pocket, machine

embroider front of pocket, placing embroidery at least $^{3}/_{4}$" below seamline of pocket.

Cut one pocket from embroidered purple nylon. Bind one long edge of mesh with fold over binding.

Fold bag piece crosswise in half and press folded edge to mark future foldline. Mark both side edges of bag 1" on either side of the fold. Open out bag piece.

Mark one 16" end of bag piece for pocket stitching by drawing 7" vertical lines on the bag up from lower edge. Starting from right side edge, mark a line at 4$^{3}/_{4}$", 8" and 12$^{1}/_{4}$" from right side edge. Also mark centerpoint of bag lower edge at seamline.

Place mesh over marked end of bag, having right side edges and bottom edges of mesh and bag even. Mesh piece will be 4" wider than bag to allow for 1" ease on each of 4 pockets. Stitch mesh to bag along $^{1}/_{2}$" seamline on right side. Place strap over mesh and bag, having right side of strap along previous seamline stitching and end of strap even with lower edge of mesh and bag. Stitch strap to bag through all 3 layers by edgestitching from lower edge up the right side of strap, beyond the pocket binding to a point 10" from lower edge. Pivot and stitch across strap, then pivot and edgestitch down left side of strap.

Make first pocket by creating a $^{1}/_{2}$" vertical tuck for ease in the mesh on left side of strap (slide the mesh over to the right 1" to make a $^{1}/_{2}$" tuck or baste a $^{1}/_{2}$" tuck the length of the pocket) and, keeping lower edges of mesh and bag even, stitch the mesh to the bag along marked line, 4$^{3}/_{4}$" from right side edge.

Make second pocket by again creating a $^{1}/_{2}$" vertical tuck in the mesh and,

keeping lower edges even, stitch the mesh to the bag along marked line 8" from the right edge.

Thread two "D" rings on unsewn end of strapping. Place right side of strap against last pocket stitching with end of strap at lower edge of bag and mesh, making sure that strap is not twisted. Stitch strap to bag through all 3 layers by edgestitching from lower edge up the right side of the strap to binding on pocket, keeping "D" rings above stitching. Pivot and stitch across strap, then pivot and edgestitch down the left side of strap. Slip "D" rings down strap and make a small tuck in the strap so that the "D" rings will lie flat. Stitch across strap above "D" ring tuck. Pivot and continue edgestitching up right side of strap to a point 10" from the lower edge of bag. Pivot and stitch across strap, then pivot and edgestitch down left side of strap to the "D" ring tuck.

Make third pocket by creating a $^{1}/_{2}$" vertical tuck for ease in the mesh end, keeping lower edges even, stitch the mesh to the bag along previously marked line 12$^{1}/_{4}$" from right edge of bag.

Make fourth pocket by again creating a $^{1}/_{2}$" vertical tuck in the mesh. The left edge of the mesh should now line up with the left edge of the bag. Keeping lower edges even, stitch mesh to bag along $^{1}/_{2}$" seamline on left side.

Make money pocket. Turn in $^{1}/_{4}$" on both ends of pocket piece to the wrong side and press. Fold pocket piece in half crosswise along foldline, right sides together. Pin. Stitch both side seams in $^{1}/_{4}$" seams. Turn pocket. Press. Baste together top pressed edges of the pocket and edgestitch together. Stitch one Velcro® dot to center top of pocket as shown on pattern.

Turn top edges of both pocket flap pieces

$^1/_4$" to the wrong side and press. Stitch the other Velcro® dot to the center of flap facing as shown on pattern. Pin flap to flap facing, right sides together and stitch curve in $^1/_4$" seam. Clip seam to accommodate curve. Turn flap. Press. Baste together top pressed edges of flap.

Mark bag for pocket placement by marking a side stitching line $^3/_8$" from the left side of the center strap, the other side stitching line $2^7/_8$" from the left side of the center strap and the bottom stitching line $^3/_8$" above the top of the pocket binding. Side lines should extend $3^1/_4$" up from the marked bottom line.

Pin pocket to bag along these lines. Edgestitch pocket to bag along the sides and lower edge of pocket. Top of pocket is $^1/_2$" wider than marked stitching lines to create ease for pocket.

Place top edge of pocket flap $^1/_4$" above top of pocket, centering flap. Edgestitch basted, pressed edges of pocket flap to bag.

Fold entire bag lengthwise, right sides together and pin side seams together. Using a zipper foot to stitch close to strap, stitch entire side seam in $^1/_2$" seam, being careful not to hit "D" rings or catch straps. Stitch just next to strap, using strap stitching as a guide. Leave side seam open for 2" (1" on either side of foldline) at previous marking. Press side seam open. Fold down facing half of bag at pressed foldline, matching lower edges. Pin. Staystitch mesh, bag and facing together, $^1/_2$" from lower edges, easing in the 1" ease of each mesh pocket as you stitch. Clip seam to staystitching every $^1/_2$", except at strap.

Pin base to bag, right sides together, matching half points of base to seam and center point of bag. Stitch bag to base inside staystitching. Serge or zigzag and trim seam.

Turn bag right side out. Edgestitch both sides of 1" opening together at top of bag. cut a 3" piece of foldover binding. Open out and press flat. Thread through hook, fold in half and baste together. To make casing on bag, turn top edge of bag to the right side of bag 1" and press.

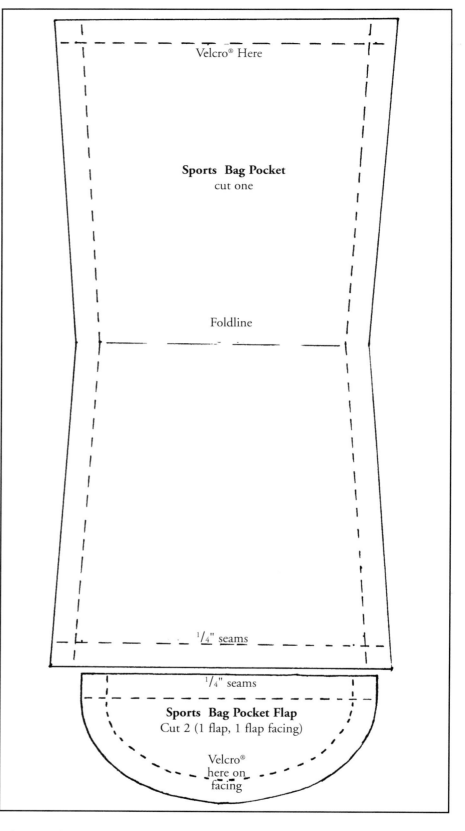

Velcro® Here

Sports Bag Pocket
cut one

Foldline

$^1/_4$" seams

$^1/_4$" seams

Sports Bag Pocket Flap
Cut 2 (1 flap, 1 flap facing)

Velcro® here on facing

Edgestitch folded edge to bag all around, sliding binding with hook into seam $1^1/_2$" from side seam on pocket side of bag. Catch in hook and continue stitching.

Thread cording through casing. Thread each end of cording through cord lock and knot ends. ❧

Designed by Tina Lewis

Delight a child with a water bottle carrier, complete with lots of pockets for toy treasures and amusements. Personalize the bag with a hand- or machine-embroidered name or add machine embroidered designs to each pocket.

This bag is sized for an 11" x 3" bottle.
SUPPLIES
$^1/_2$ yd. blue sport nylon for bag
$^3/_8$ yd. yellow sport nylon for pockets
$^1/_8$ yd. clear soft vinyl for pockets
$^1/_8$ yd. red sport nylon for binding
One star appliqué
1 yd. $^1/_8$" nylon or elastic cording
One double cord lock
Threads for embroidery

Cut one 15" x 22" piece of blue nylon for bag. Cut one $9^1/_2$" x 15" piece of yellow nylon for pockets. Cut one $3^3/_4$" x 20" piece of vinyl for pockets. Cut $1^3/_4$" x 20" piece of red nylon for pocket binding. Cut two $5^1/_2$" circles ($^1/_2$" seam allowance included) of yellow nylon for base and baste together as one. Mark the two half points on base.

Fold blue bag piece in half crosswise and

press in fold for future foldline marking. Mark along side seamlines a 2" opening, 1" on either side of fold on both sides. Mark centerpoint of lower edge of bag at seamline. Open out bag.

Fold yellow pocket piece in half lengthwise and press in fold for future foldline marking. Mark pocket stitching lines along folded yellow piece from the fold down to the lower edge of piece. Working from right side, mark lines at $3^1/_2$", $6^1/_2$", $9^1/_2$" and $12^1/_2$" from right side edge. Completed bag will have four pockets, each 3" wide, and one pocket 2" wide .

Open out yellow pocket piece. Embroider name or designs by hand or machine on a line $^7/_8$" below fold, centered between any of the pocket lines. After embroidering, re-fold yellow piece.

To make a double fold, straight grain binding for pockets, fold both long sides of red binding piece to center and press. Fold in half and press again. Encase one long edge of vinyl piece in red binding, and edgestitch binding in place with black thread.

Place folded, embroidered yellow pocket piece on one 15" end of blue bag piece, having side and lower edges even. Pin in place.

Layer bound vinyl pocket piece over yellow and blue pieces, having right side edge and lower edges even. Vinyl piece will be 5" longer than bag and yellow pocket to allow 1" ease for each of 5 pockets. Staystitch all three layers together along right side seam $^1/_2$" from edge. Slide just the vinyl piece to the right 1" to create a $^1/_2$" tuck in vinyl.

Keeping lower edges even, stitch with black thread along first pocket line $3^1/_2$" from right side, stitching both yellow pocket and vinyl pocket pieces to the bag.

Repeat tucking vinyl and stitching pocket for second, third and fourth pockets. Finally, bring left edge of vinyl even with left side edge of bag and yellow pocket and staystitch along left side seamline $^1/_2$" from edge.

Fold entire bag lengthwise, right sides together and pin side seams together. Stitch entire side seam in $^1/_2$" seam, stitching just inside previous pocket staystitching. Leave side seam open for 2" (1" on either side of foldline at previous marking). Press seam open. Fold down facing half of bag at pressed foldline, matching all lower edges. Pin. Using a long stitch, staystitch vinyl, yellow pocket bag and facing together $^1/_2$" from lower edges, tucking vinyl ease into two $^1/_4$" tucks along each pocket lower edge as you stitch. Clip seam to staystitching every $^1/_2$".

Pin base to bag, right sides together, matching half points of base to seam and centerpoint of bag. Stitch bag to base just inside staystitching. Stitch again $^1/_4$" from seam and zigzag or serge seam.

Turn bag right side out. Using black thread, edgestitch both sides of 1" opening together at top of bag. To make casing, turn top folded edge of bag to right side of bag 1" and press. With black thread, edgestitch folded edge to the bag all around.

Stitch appliqué star to the bag, centered $1^1/_2$" above top of yellow pockets, centered at a pocket stitching line.

Thread cord through casing. Knot ends securely and ease back through casing so that knotted end is hidden. Thread looped end of cord through cord lock and knot looped end. ❧

The Jester's Bag

Shown on page 62

Designed by Tina Lewis

Perfect for New Year's Eve or any festive occasion, the Jester's Bag uses glitzy fabric scraps and touches of embellishment to make a delightful hostess gift or centerpiece.

This bag is sized for $12^1/_2$" x $3^1/_2$" bottle.
SUPPLIES
$^5/_8$ yd. black velvet
$2^1/_2$ yds. gold metallic cording
4 gold tassels
7 gold jingle bells
7 scraps of brightly colored satin, metallic or novelty fabrics
Embellishments: various beads, sequins, ribbons, braids, metallic threads, etc.

Cut one $15^1/_2$" x 19" velvet piece for bag. Cut one circle $5^3/_4$" in diameter ($^1/_2$" seam allowance included) of velvet for base of bag. Cut seven collar pieces of seven different fabric scraps.

Arrange the seven cut collar pieces in a pleasing order and stitch each piece to the next along the $^1/_4$" side seams to make one long piece, making sure points are in the same direction, Press all seams open.

Turn long straight edge of collar under $^1/_4$" and press.

Embellish this multicolored, pointed collar piece with beads, sequins, appliques, hand or machine embroidery or crazy quilt stitches along the seam lines. Embroider "Happy New Year" on one of the points, if desired, by hand or machine. Keep beads and sequins within seam allowance on the points to allow for turning. End embellishments $1^1/_2$" from pressed edge to allow for casing.

For one casing opening, work a 1" vertical buttonhole in the center of the $15^1/_2$" bag width, between $10^1/_2$" and $11^1/_2$" up from the lower edge. Staystitch $^1/_2$" from lower edge. Clip to staystitching every $^1/_2$". Mark center of lower edge.

Center embellished collar piece right side down on the right side of prepared bag, having points of collar touch along the top edge of the bag. Pin. Baste $^1/_4$" from edge all around the points to prevent shifting on velvet. Using a small stitch, stitch points all around in $^1/_4$" seam, pivoting cleanly at inner and outer corners of points and starting and stopping at $^1/_4$" seamlines at sides. Trim velvet to $^1/_4$" seams following collar. Clip all inner corners. Trim all points. Clip side seams to stitching at seam line. Carefully turn collar, working out points.

Baste close to edges. Press.

With right sides together, bring side seams together, opening out collar. Pin, matching collar seam. For the other casing opening, mark a 1" opening along side seam between $10^1/_2$" and $11^1/_2$" up from the lower edge. Stitch side seams in $^1/_4$" seam along the length of the bag and collar, leaving open between casing markings and being careful not to catch in collar points. Finish each seam allowance by serging or zigzagging. Press seam open.

Turn collar back on bag. Embellish last collar seam, if desired. To form casing, pin and then edgestitch pressed edge of collar to bag all around. Stitch again 1" away from edgestitching. Seam opening and buttonhole should be centered within casing lines on the right side.

Mark half points on base piece. Pin base to bag, right sides together, matching seam to one half point on base and center mark of long edge to the other. Stitch bag to base in $^1/_2$" seam. Trim seam to $^1/_4$". Serge or zigzag seams together.

Turn bag right side out. Stitch bells to collar points. Cut cord in half, wrapping cut ends with tape. Draw one cord through casing and out same opening. Draw second cord through casing on opposite side and out the same opening. Trim cords to desired length. Stitch cord ends to tassels. ❧

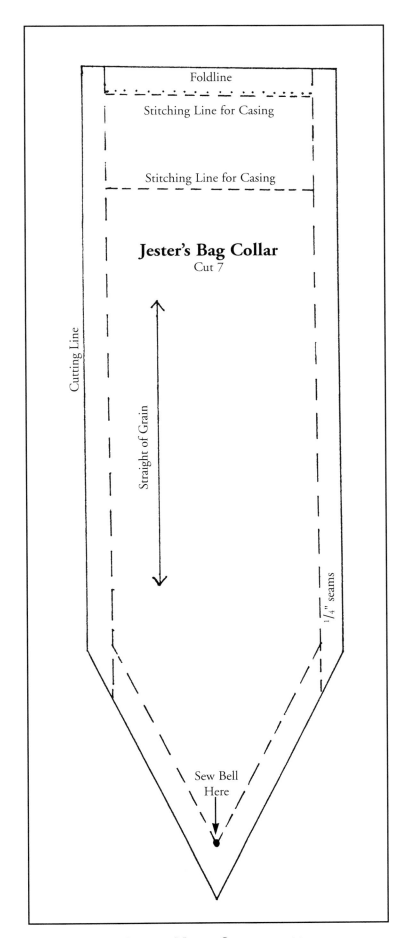

Foldline

Stitching Line for Casing

Stitching Line for Casing

Jester's Bag Collar
Cut 7

Cutting Line

Straight of Grain

¼" seams

Sew Bell Here

Designed by Tina Lewis

Present a special bottle of wine or a sparkling beverage in a jolly Santa Bag, sure to bring a smile and become a welcome addition to any Christmas decor.

Bag is sized for a 13^1/$_2$" x 3" bottle.

SUPPLIES

^{1}/$_2$ yd. red felt
1 yd. white ^{3}/$_8$" cable cord
^{1}/$_2$ yd. 1" wide red grosgrain ribbon
Scraps of pink, white and green felt
Three red jingle bells
One 1" white pom-pom
DMC embroidery floss:
   Black 310
   Red 304

Cut a 14" x 18" piece of red felt. Cut one 5^3/$_8$" circle (^{1}/$_2$" seam allowance included) of red felt.

Use diagram of Santa appliqué to trace patterns for the following pieces: face, beard, cap, cap fur, mustache, nose and holly. Follow dotted lines to add underlap allowance to face, beard and cap pieces. Cut beard, cap fur and mustache of white felt, face of pink, cap and nose of red and holly of green. Transfer markings for eyes and mouth.

Assemble Santa face following diagram by slipping face underlap under beard. With 3 strands of black 310 floss, edgestitch beard to face with tiny running stitches. Embroider eyes with 3 stands of black using a backstitch. Stitch nose to face, then layer mustache over nose and stitch. Embroider mouth with satin stitch using 2 strands of red 304. Set aside.

To shape top of bag, place cuff pattern piece on top of 14" x 18" bag piece, having point of beard touching the top edge of felt and the side edge of pattern piece lined up against side edge of felt. Recut the shape of top of bag, following pattern, cutting around the V of the beard and continuing straight across the width of the bag beyond the pattern piece. Side seams should now measure 16".

Place assembled Santa face on the cuff, having edge of beard ^{1}/$_8$" inside the newly shaped top edges of bag. Pin. Edgestitch beard to cuff. Place cap fur on face and slip cap under cap fur, following diagram. Pin. Edgestitch cap fur and cap to cuff.

Add holly leaf as indicated and stitch edge and center. Stitch bells at tip of holly. Stitch pom-pom to point of cap.

To make casing, cut a 14" length of ribbon. Press ends in ^{1}/$_2$". Pin ribbon to wrong side of bag (the side with the Santa face) having the lower edge of the ribbon parallel to and 8^3/$_4$" up from the lower edge of the bag. Center ribbon so that the folded ends are ^{1}/$_2$" from sides of the bag. Thread machine with red thread, and edgestitch both long sides of ribbon to bag.

Staystitch lower edge of bag ^{1}/$_2$" from edge. Clip to stitching every ^{1}/$_2$". Mark centerpoint of lower edge.

Bring bag side seams together, right side facing. Pin. Stitch in a ^{1}/$_4$" seam from the base of the bag to the ribbon casing. Leave a 1" opening in the seam in line with the ribbon. Continue stitching above the casing for 2". Clip seam to top of stitching. Turn bag right side out. With wrong sides together, stitch remaining ^{1}/$_4$" side seam. Fold ^{1}/$_4$" seam allowances open flat to the bag at casing opening and slip stitch in place, being careful not to catch in the casings.

Pin circle base to bag, right sides together, matching half points on base to seam and centerpoint of bag. Stitch base to bag in ^{1}/$_2$" seam. Stitch again ^{1}/$_4$" from seam. Trim to stitching.

Thread cording through casing. Trim to desired length and knot ends. ❧

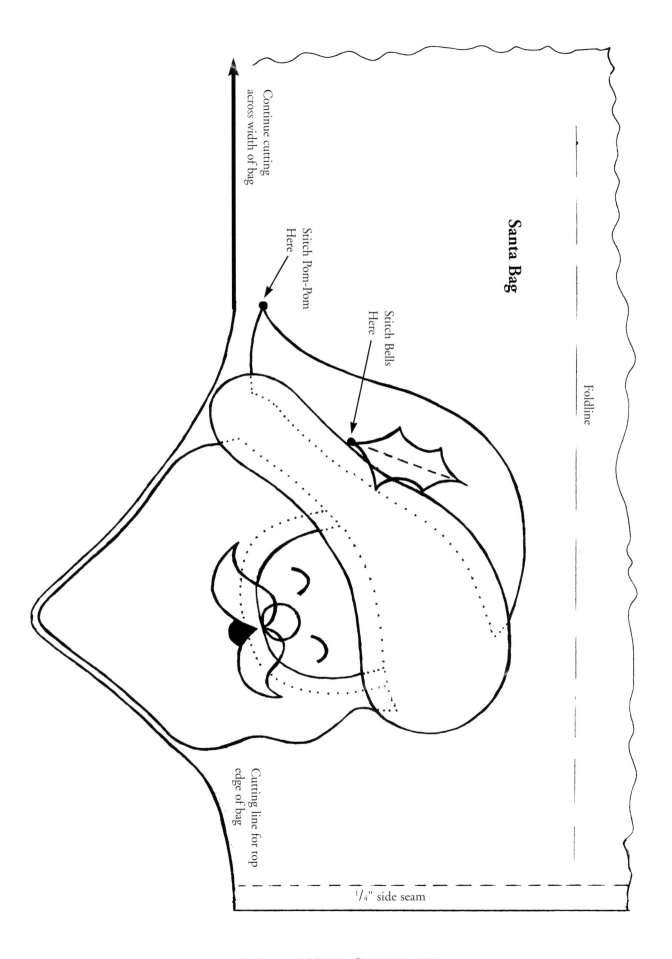

Santa Bag

Foldline

Continue cutting
across width of bag

Stitch Pom-Pom
Here

Stitch Bells
Here

Cutting line for top
edge of bag

¹/₄" side seam

Snowman Bag *Shown on page 63*

Designed by Tina Lewis

Spread good cheer with the Snowman Bag made of wool melton, scraps of felt and folk art charm. This decorative bag could also be filled with holiday candles, homemade preserves or other special gifts.

This bag is sized for a 11¹/₂" x 3" bottle.

SUPPLIES
¹/₂ yd. dark blue wool melton or felt
¹/₄ yd. white felt
Scraps of black, red, green and gold felt
DMC Floss:
    Red 304   Orange 722
    Black 310   White
Ten ¹/₄" to ³/₈" assorted sew through
    buttons in bright colors for tree
Three ¹/₄" black shank buttons for
    snowman
¹/₂ yd. 1" dark blue grosgrain ribbon
1¹/₄ yd. ¹/₄" white cable cording

Cut a 13¹/₂" x 14" piece of wool melton or felt for bag. Cut snow, snowman and a

5¹/₄" circle (¹/₂" seam allowance included) of white felt. Transfer words to snow and markings to snowman. Cut hat of black felt. Cut scarf of red felt. Cut tree and holly of green felt. Cut moon of gold felt.

Place snow along the lower 14" edge of blue bag piece, having lower edges even. Baste in place, slightly easing snow on bag to allow for curve of finished bag. Using 3 strands of black floss, blanket stitch top edge of snow to bag with ¹/₄" stitches, ¹/₄" apart.

Using a backstitch and 3 strands of black floss, embroider "Be of Good Cheer." Trim blue bag behind snow to ³/₄" from lower edge. Staystitch lower edge of snow ¹/₂" from lower edge. Clip to stitching every ¹/₂". Mark center point of lower edge at seamline.

Embroider details on snowman. Eyes are 6-strand black French knots. Nose is satin stitched in orange using 2 strands. Mouth is 4-strand black French knots. Sew 3 buttons as indicated.

Pin snowman to bag as indicated on snow pattern. Using 3 strands of black floss, blanket stitch snowman to bag using ¹/₈" stitches, ¹/₈" apart.

Pin hat to snowman. Blanket stitch edges, same as snowman. Tack holly leaves to hat and secure with three 4-strand red French knots.

Fold scarf at an angle. Set fold at snowman's neck and with six strands of red, backstitch around neck, catching in scarf. Fringe ends of scarf.

Pin tree to bag as indicated on snow pattern. Blanket stitch edges, same as

snowman. Sew buttons to tree with black floss.

Pin moon to bag, centered between tree and snowman, 5" below top of bag. Blanket stitch in place, same as snowman.

Randomly cross stitch snowflakes in the "sky" using 6 strands of white floss. Stitch snowflakes only to 3¹/₂" from top of bag.

To make casing, cut grosgrain ribbon to 14". Turn ends in ¹/₂" and press. Pin ribbon to wrong side of bag, having lower edge of ribbon parallel to and 3³/₄" down from the top edge of the bag. Center ribbon so that the folded ends are ¹/₂" from side edges of the bag. With matching blue thread, edgestitch both long sides of the ribbon to the bag.

Fold bag lengthwise, right sides together and pin side seams. Stitch side seams in ¹/₄" seam, leaving a 1" opening in the seam in line with the ribbon casing. Whip seam allowances open from lower edge of ribbon to top edge of bag, being careful not to catch in the casings.

Using 3 strands of black floss, blanket stitch top edge of bag with ¹/₄" stitches, ¹/₄" apart.

Pin base to bag, right sides together, matching half points on base to seam and centerpoint of bag. Stitch bag to base, inside staystitching, in ¹/₂" seam. Stitch again ¹/₄" from seam. Trim to stitching.

Turn bag right side out. Thread cording through casing. Tie in a bow and trim to desired length. Knot ends and fringe cording below knots. ❧

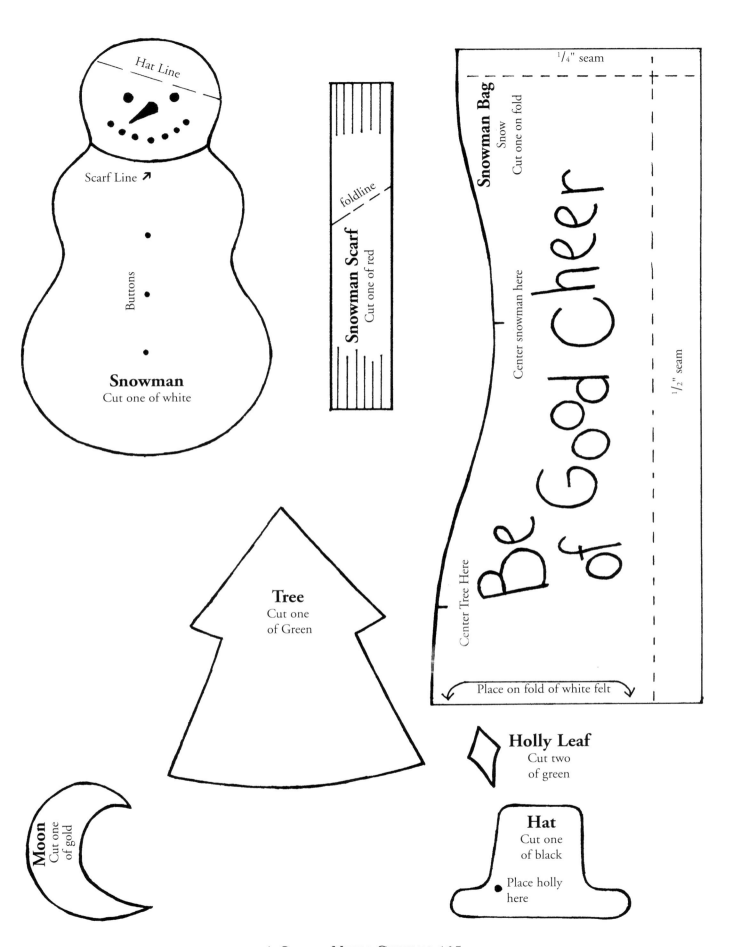

Hat Line

Scarf Line ↗

Buttons

Snowman
Cut one of white

Snowman Scarf
Cut one of red

foldline

1/4" seam

Snowman Bag
Snow
Cut one on fold

Center snowman here

Be of Good Cheer

1/2" seam

Center Tree Here

Tree
Cut one
of Green

Place on fold of white felt

Holly Leaf
Cut two
of green

Moon
Cut one
of gold

Hat
Cut one
of black

Place holly
here

The Cuffed Bag *Shown on page 63*

Designed by Tina Lewis

The shaped cuff of this candy striped bag is ideal for one of the many computer-generated embroidery designs available on today's sewing machines. Hand embroidery or even holiday appliqués could be substituted.

This bag is sized for a 12" x 3" bottle.

SUPPLIES
$5/8$ yd. red and white striped cotton
$5/8$ yd. medium weight white cotton
$1/2$ yd. red and white striped piping
$1/2$ yd. gold metallic piping
$1^1/2$ yds. $1/4$" gold metallic cording

One red tassel
Gold metallic thread
Threads for machine embroidery

Make pattern piece for bag by adding 11" to the pattern where indicated. Fold red and white striped fabric on the bias. Cut one bag piece of red and white striped fabric, having pattern fold line on the bias fold of the fabric.

Make a whole pattern piece by tracing pattern onto a folded piece of tissue. Transfer pattern cutting lines to white fabric and work machine embroidery, centering design on cuff facing point, before cutting pattern piece. Cut one bag lining piece of embroidered white cotton.

Cut one $5^1/2$" circle ($1/2$" seam allowance included) of red and white stripe and one of white. Baste wrong sides together.

Stitch metallic piping to striped piping so that metallic fabric sits snugly inside stripe, creating a double piping. Pin piping to shaped edge of white cuff, right sides together, having piping stitching along $1/2$" seamline. Using a zipper foot, stitch piping to cuff in a $1/2$" seam, clipping cording to stitching at point in order to pivot and tapering piping into seam allowance $1/2$" from side edges.

Place bag over corded white lining, right

sides together. Pin along cuff edge. Stitch bag to lining, following previous cording stitching. Trim point. Turn right side out and press.

Open out lining and match cross seams. With right sides together, pin entire bag and lining back seam. Stitch seam in $1/2$" seam allowance. Press seam open. Turn lining down over bag.

Pin lining to bag matching lower edges. Staystitch bag and lining together $1/2$" from lower edges. Clip to stitching every $1/2$". Mark center front point of bag at seamline.

Pin prepared base to bag, right sides together, matching center back of base to back seam of bag and center front to centerpoint of bag. Stitch bag to base in $1/2$" seam. Serge or stitch again $1/4$" from previous stitching and trim.

Turn bag right side out. Fold down cuff at foldline. Wrap tassel with gold metallic thread, if desired. Stitch tassel to point of cuff.

Wrap cording around bag, tie a bow, and trim to desired length. Knot ends of cording and trim. ❧

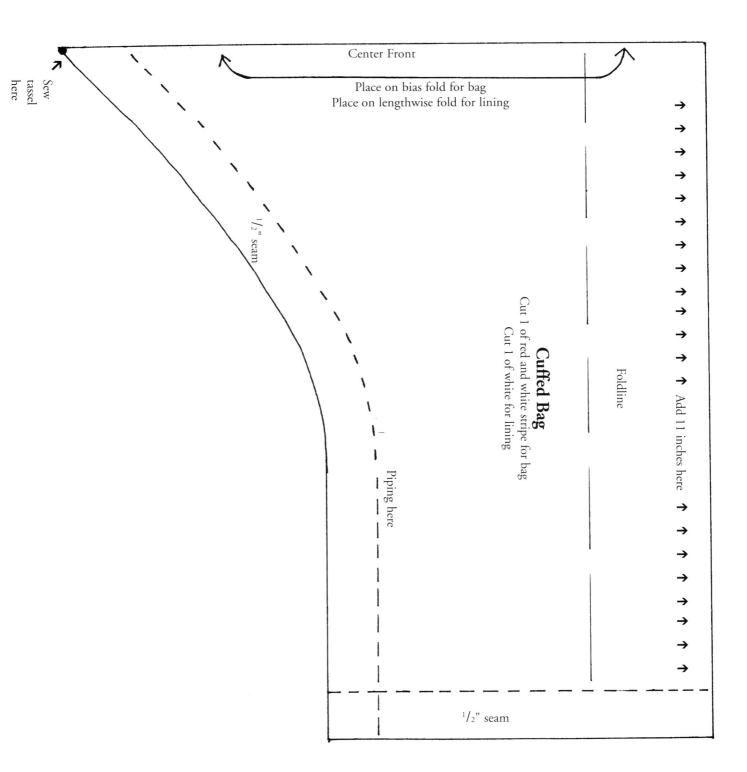

Center Front

Place on bias fold for bag
Place on lengthwise fold for lining

Sew tassel here

¹/₂" seam

Cuffed Bag
Cut 1 of red and white stripe for bag
Cut 1 of white for lining

Foldline

Add 11 inches here

Piping here

¹/₂" seam

Designed by Tina Lewis

A wonderful gift for a special teacher, co-worker, teammate or family member, the clear vinyl Candy Bag can also be filled with any homemade treat. The smockpatch "tag" is a Christmas ornament that may be personalized with a greeting or date written in fabric pen on the back. The bag itself makes a charming serving dish to display during the holidays.

SUPPLIES
$^1/_3$ yd. clear, soft vinyl
$2^1/_4$ yds. purchased or handmade $^1/_4$" cording
$^3/_4$ yd. purchased or handmade $^1/_4$" double fold bias binding
Scrap of fabric for casing
Clear nylon thread

Cut a $22^1/_2$" x $9^1/_2$" piece of vinyl for bag. Cut a circle 8" in diameter ($^1/_2$" seam allowance included) of vinyl for base of bag. Cut two 12" x $2^1/_4$" pieces of fabric for casing.

Using the scallop template and starting and stopping the template at $^1/_4$" side

seamlines, draw 7 scallops along top edge of vinyl bag piece, having scallops touch the edge. Cut scallops.

Mark $^1/_2$" seamline along opposite lower edge of vinyl bag piece and clip to seamline every $^1/_2$". Mark center point of lower edge.

Fold bag piece crosswise to bring side seams together and using clear nylon thread and a longer stitch, stitch $^1/_4$" side seam. Do not backtack on vinyl, since too many stitches too close together will slash vinyl. Knot threads instead.

Fold bias binding over scalloped top edge of bag and edgestitch binding to bag, working slowly and easing or stretching binding around scallops. Tuck binding ends in $^1/_4$" and slipstitch together by hand.

Turn ends of each casing piece $^1/_2$" to wrong side and press. Turn long sides of each casing piece in $^1/_2$" and press so that each casing piece is 11" x $1^1/_4$". Mark center point of one casing piece. Set this piece on the outside of the bag, having upper edge of casing $2^1/_8$" below the top of the scallops and center of casing at center back bag seam. Edgestitch both long sides of casing to bag, leaving ends open. Set second casing piece on outside of bag front, having upper edge of casing $2^1/_8$" below top of scallops and ends lined up with first casing piece. Edgestitch both long sides of second casing to bag, leaving ends open.

Mark center front and back of base piece. Working with the bag inside out, match center front and back of base piece to centerpoint and back seam of right side of bag. Stitch bag to base all around. Stitch again $^1/_4$" from seam and trim seam close to stitching. Turn bag right side out. Cut cording in half. Draw one piece of cording through casing, around

and out the same opening. Draw second piece of cording through opposite opening, around and out the same opening. Knot cord ends at desired length. Tuck in ends of cord and stitch closed by hand.

SMOCKPATCH ORNAMENT SUPPLIES
$^1/_4$ yd. fabric for smocking
Scrap of fabric for ornament
Scrap of fusible interfacing
Scrap of fusible fleece
DMC embroidery floss:

Red 304	Flesh 353
Green 699	Black 310
Gold 680	Brown 898
Blue 793	White

Pleat a 4" x 15" piece of fabric in 9 rows. Tie off 48 pleats (28 pleats for Santa and 10 pleats allowed on either side). Backsmock every row with 2 strands of floss which matches fabric.

Work "Santa's Walk" following graph, using 4 strands of floss unless otherwise indicated. Start on Row 5, 12 pleats from left side, with a down cable.

LEGEND
304 (red) – robe, hat, mouth, gift in sack
353 (flesh) – face
White – beard, fur and topknot
699 (green) – tree in sack
310 (black) – boots, glove, buttons
680 (gold) – walking stick and gifts in sack
898 (brown) – sack
793 (blue) – eye and gifts in sack

Topknot is a French knot in white, 6 strands. Buttons are French knots in black 310, 4 strands. Eye is French knot in blue 793, 2 strands. Mouth is a tiny straight stitch in red 304, 2 strands. Gifts are French knots in gold 680, 4 strands. Tree is worked in stem stitch with straight stitch branches in green 699, 3 strands. Walking stick is worked in stem stitch in gold 680, 4 strands, along line indicated, interrupted by the stitches of the glove.

To make the ornament, transfer shape of ornament line for window and embroidery design for front of ornament to fabric. Transfer shape of ornament for back to fabric. Work embroidery on front before cutting out. With 3 strands of floss, embroider "JOY" in white using a double stem stitch. Embroider holly leaves in green 699 in satin stitch (3 strands) and holly series in 4 strands of red 304 French knots. Cut out front piece and a front piece of fusible fleece. Fuse fleece to wrong side of fabric, then cut out window. Prepare back by cutting out back piece and a back piece of interfacing. Fuse interfacing to wrong side of fabric.

Sew finished front window over smocking, centering design. Baste. From back, trim off smocking to within ¹/₈" from outer edge of front piece. On right side, satin stitch frame to smocking around window, covering edge. Set smocked piece on back, wrong sides together. Baste. Satin stitch around outer edge of ornament. Add a loop of thread to hang. 🐝

Smockpatch Ornament

Cut one for back
Cut one with opening for front

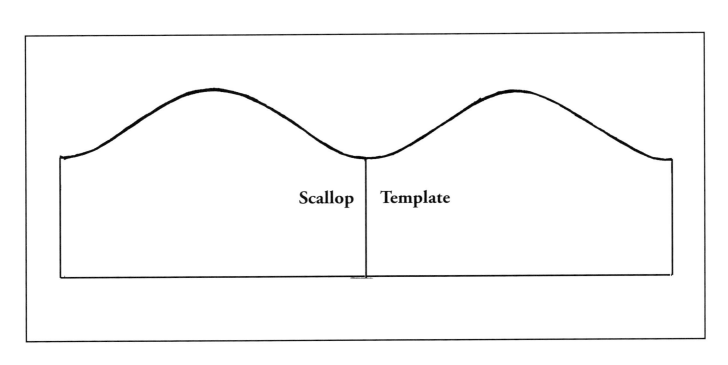

Scallop   Template

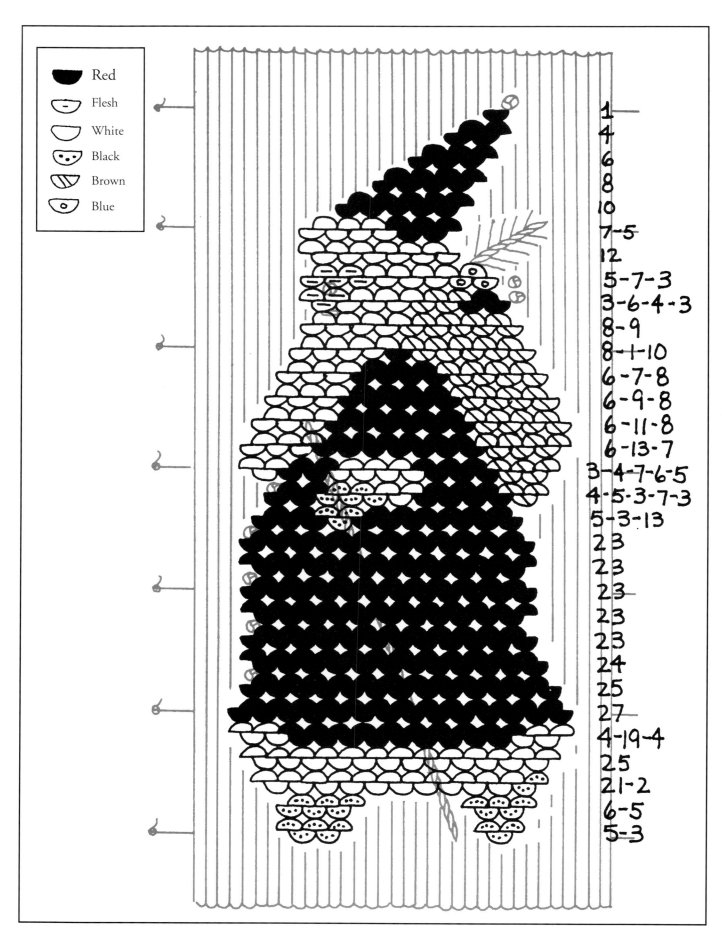

Legend

Symbol	Color
●	Red
⌣	Flesh
⌣	White
⊙	Black
⌣	Brown
⊙	Blue

1
4
6
8
10
7-5
12
5-7-3
3-6-4-3
8-9
8-1-10
6-7-8
6-9-8
6-11-8
6-13-7
3-4-7-6-5
4-5-3-7-3
5-3-13
23
23
23
23
23
24
25
27
4-19-4
25
21-2
6-5
5-3

Smocked Round Collar

Cotton velveteen dress is "Collar Dress;" smocking design is "First Communion," both by Oliver-Goodin & Co. Patterns available at fine needlework shops. See Resource Guide.

Most round-necked dress patterns will accommodate a smocked collar. Other smocking designs may also be used. General instructions for a round collar follow.

GENERAL INSTRUCTIONS
A smocked collar is an easy way to add elegance to any holiday dress. Extend the usefulness and versatility of the collar by making it detachable.

SUPPLIES
$^3/_8$ yd. Swiss batiste
$1^3/_4$ yds. lace edging
$1^3/_4$ lace insertion
$1^3/_4$ yds. entredeux

Cut fabric 44" long by desired width (3" to 5" inches, depending on size of collar). For larger sizes (4 and up), French seam two strips of fabric together, or cut 60" lengthwise. Pleat desired number of rows using a pleater or dot transfer sheet. Finish collar edge by rolling and whipping both ends and one long side of batiste. Attach entredeux, lace insertion, and lace edging. Miter lace at corners. (Collar pictured has vertical strips of lace insertion stitched to batiste before pleating, and smocking is worked between lace strips. Additional lace is required for this style.)

Using dress neckline as a template, place pleated collar piece on guide and adjust pleats to form circle. Mark center front pleat; tie off pleating threads. Choose a smocking design suitable for bishop dresses, where lower rows include wave or trellis stitches (which allow collar to lie smoothly on garment).

With a lengthened machine stitch, sew $^1/_8$" above first row of smocking.

Attach collar following pattern instructions. To make a detachable collar, attach a narrow bias neck band to collar neck edge. Stich a button loop and shank button at back closing, or fasten with beauty pins. ❧

Lace Jabot *Shown on page 69*

Designed by Trudy Horne

Underdress and Waistcoat are "Ashley's 2-in-1 Dress" by Deborah's Designs. Pattern available at fine needlework shops. See Resource Guide.

This design is adaptable to most round necklines.

SUPPLIES
Jabot, dickey and stand-up collar pattern on Pull-out
$1/2$ yd. organdy or similar fabric for jabot and stand-up collar
$1/3$ yd. fabric for dickey
$1^3/4$ yd. lace edging
$1^1/8$ yd. entredeux

STITCH GUIDE
Red 304: Bow (shadow work); flower petals (satin stitch)
Yellow 744: Flower centers (French knots)
Dk. Green 319: Vines (outline stitch)
Lt. Green 368: Leaves (satin stitch)

INSTRUCTIONS
Jabot
1. Trace outline and embroidery design onto jabot fabric with a soft graphite pencil. Machine staystitch along broken lines.

2. Embroider shadow work bow on one side of fabric; work surface stitches on the other side.

3. Cut out jabot along solid line. Cut out jabot facing. Stitch, right sides together, along unnotched edge. Trim seam allowance to $1/8$".

4. Turn right side out. Whip entredeux and slightly gathered lace edging to edge.

5. Baste top edges together and gather to measure $1^3/4$" to 2". Machine stitch over gathers to hold in place.

TIP: When adding any trim to a faced piece, stitch from the underside (facing side), catching facing fabric only with each stitch. Whipping stitches will be almost invisible from right side, especially if fine sewing thread and a small needle are used.

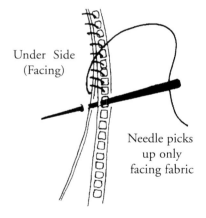

Under Side (Facing)

Needle picks up only facing fabric

Illustration 1

Dickey
6. Cut out dickey. Fusible interfacing may be applied to wrong side if fabric is flimsy. Clean finish outer edge of dickey with zigzag or overlock. Turn under at back edges. Staystitch seamline of neck. Clip neck edge allowance to staystitching at 1" intervals.

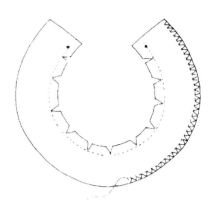

Illustration 2

Baste jabot to dickey, matching center fronts.

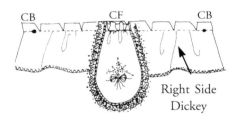

CB   CF   CB

Right Side Dickey

Illustration 3

Stand-up Collar
7. Cut out collar and collar facing. Right sides together, stitch unnotched edges of collar to facing, stopping and starting at dots. Trim seam allowance to $1/4$" from dot to dot. Turn right side out and press.

Illustration 4

8. Pin and baste right side of collar to right side of dickey, matching center fronts, notches and dots. Stitch, being careful not to sew collar facing into seam.

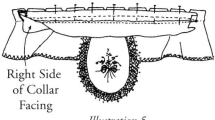

Right Side
of Collar
Facing

Illustration 5

Trim seam allowances and clip curve. Press seam away from dickey. Turn right side out and press.

Turn under free edge of collar facing and whip to machine stitching.

9. Try jabot/collar/dickey on wearer and mark closing. Turn under ends of dickey at back so that the right side overlaps left. Sew small pearl shank buttons on left side, and work button loops on right side of collar.

The dickey can be tacked to inside of jacket, or simply tucked underneath when worn.

THE FIVE PETAL FLOWER

The five petal flower can be worked using lazy daisy stitch, or two bullion knots (called a bullion leaf). For rich texture and luster, padded satin stitch offers the most impressive results.

For padding underneath the satin stitch, use a small needle (#12 sharp) and one strand of floss. It is not necessary to tie off between each petal in a flower. Proper alignment of the grouping of petals helps to perfect this delicate flower. Practice stitch on a scrap of fabric.

EXECUTING THE STITCH

1. To begin the first petal, bring thread from wrong side up through bottom (narrow end) of petal. Do not pull thread all the way through. Leave a 1-2" tail underneath.

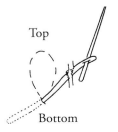

Top

Bottom

Illustration 6

This tail is held in place and caught in the stitches underneath. Clip any extra thread when all petals are completed.

Work lazy daisy stitch.

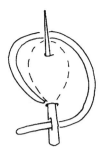

Illustration 7

Illustration 8

Place one straight stitch inside the lazy daisy.

Illustration 9

2. Come up from wrong side at bottom of petal and begin satin stitch, working from bottom of petal to top (wider end). Pick up only a thread or two of fabric at the bottom, gradually picking up more

fabric toward the top. The finished length of the petal should be no greater than $1/8$".

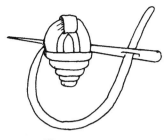

Illustration 10

3. When one petal is completed, sink needle to wrong side. Slide needle under stitches on the wrong side and go to the next petal, beginning as in Step 1, except that no tail will be needed to begin.

4. Complete as many petals as thread length will allow. Work French knots in centers of flowers. If eyelets are used instead of French knots, they should be worked before the petals.

Note: Work leaves on vines in same manner as petals.

Symmetry is important when working the five petal flower. To ensure proper alignment, make sure each petal is directly across from a space.

Illustration 11

To do this, lay working needle over center of each petal. If the needle does not point to a space (see Illustration 12), then petal placement must be adjusted. It isn't necessary to redraw petals which are misaligned; simply work petal in proper position. Any pencil markings that show will wash out. ❧

Illustration 12

Shadow Work Designs *Shown on pages 70 & 71*

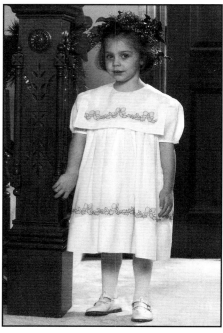

Black velvet jumpsuit is "Steger" by Oliver-Goodin & Co. Green velvet jjumpsuit is "Unisex Knickers" by Cindy Foose (available from Creative Needle). Collar pattern is from "Steger." White dress is a variation of "Virginia" from Oliver-Goodin & Co. Patterns available at fine needlework shops. See Resource Guide.

All three shadow work designs on Pattern Pull-out. See "Shadow Work Basics" for embroidery instructions. DMC floss was used for embroidery, in colors to complement fabric.

Note: Repeat elements in inner portion of holly design as needed to fit collar, with bows placed at corners. In design with bows and candy canes, reverse bows for opposite corners. 🔔

Bear - Rum - Pa - Pum - Pum *Shown on page 72*

Designed by Delbra W. Moore

SUPPLIES
Purchased sweater
DMC Floss:

310 Black	435 Brown
991 Green	712 Cream
400 Rust	820 Blue
823 Dk. Blue	738 Tan

Metallic Gold Ribbon Floss®
Gold thread
Gold beads

GAUGE: The sweater pictured is bulky, 4 stitches by 6 rows gauge. Finer (more stitches and rows per inch) gauges will result in a smaller bear. Twelve strands of DMC embroidery floss were used throughout the design. Finer gauges require fewer strands.

SIZE ADJUSTMENT: To end up with a bear the size pictured on a different sweater gauge, trace around edges of graph to make a paper pattern or template. Cut out and trace with thread or water soluble marker on sweater. Simply fill the resulting drawn outline with duplicate stitch. The bear figure is not symmetrical, so working it from a drawing rather than the graph is easy.

CENTERING: Match bear's center with center front of sweater. Place bear high enough on sweater so that none of the bear is hidden in folds of sweater hem.

DETAIL
Hat Band—Stitched in metallic ribbon

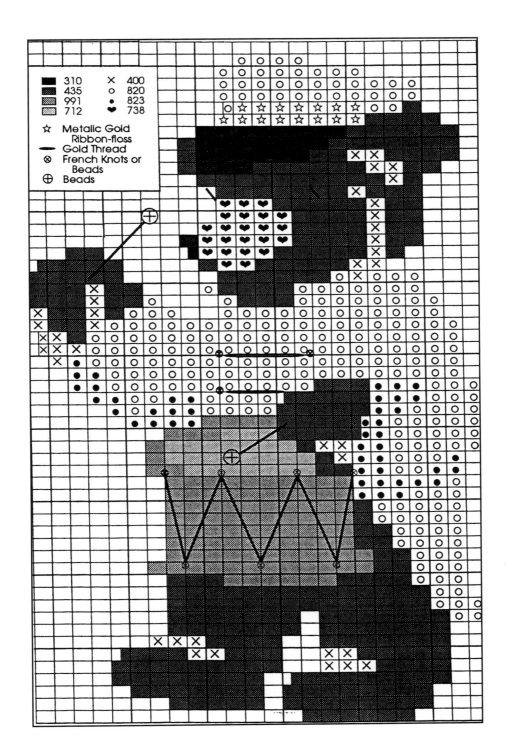

floss. Dip cut ends of ribbon floss in seam sealant to prevent raveling. Adjust tension to assure sufficient coverage.

Eyes—Thread needle with one length each white and black floss. Angle straight stitches as directed on graph to get a "friendly" look in face.

Mouth—Outline lighter portion of nose with back stitch in DMC 400 rust to accent mouth.

Brass Buttons—Chest stripes are stitched in same gold metallic ribbon floss used on hat band. Buttons are small gold tone beads. Stitch with hand-sewing thread matching coat color. Notice that one button is hidden behind paw.

Drum Sticks—Use either straight stitches or long bugle beads as shown. Head of stick is round gold bead. A circlet bullion may be substituted.

Drum—Two strands of cream floss are couched for drum strings. Place according to graph. Top of each angle is anchored with a circlet bullion. Small beads may be substituted. 🦋

Shadow Work Santa

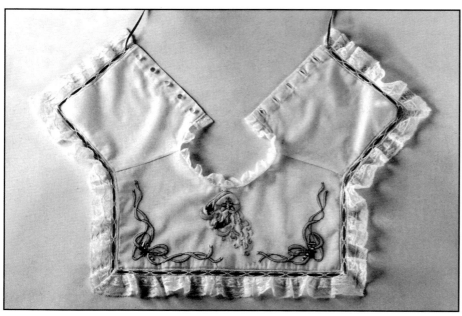

Designed by Jody B. Raines

SUPPLIES

Embroidery design on Pull-out
DMC Floss:

White	Black
Red 321	Green 699
Blue 827	Brown 780
Flesh 754	Pink 335
Blue 798	Grey 415

#26 tapestry needle, or #10, 11, or 12
   crewel needle
Sheer white batiste or similar fabric
   (pattern yardage requirements plus $^1/_2$
   yd. extra
Embroidery hoop
Sharp pencil
Square collar pattern of your choice
Check pattern requirements for
   entredeux, beading and lace edging
Red glass beads and three or four small
   white buttons (depending on collar
   size)

INSTRUCTIONS

Prewash, press and starch fabric. Trace
collar outline using a water soluble
marker. Reduce or enlarge design on a
copier to fit the size of collar you have
selected. Cut a larger rectangle of fabric,
allowing ample space around front collar
outline to easily move embroidery hoop
as you work.

With a sharp pencil, trace entire design in
a light fine line. Remember to leave an
inch between neck and Santa's head to
accommodate entredeux and lace edgings.

Since very sheer batiste tends to pull in
an embroidery hoop, cut a 2" doughnut
of interfacing to fit your hoop and use it
to stabilize material for embroidery.

See "Shadow Work Basics" for
embroidery instructions.

STITCHING ORDER

Santa's Eyes: Make a small black pupil
by creating a half circle of back stitches
and filling in with tiny satin stitches. For
the iris, make a larger blue half-circle
around pupil. For larger sizes, add two
white stitches on top of pupils, either on
left or right of each, for highlights.

Outline eye in black back stitches which
set in top of iris and underline the half
circle as illustrated. (Illustration 1 on
Pull-out.) Taper outer lines for laugh
creases. Weave floss several times through
stitches on back and clip excess thread
tails so they won't show when flesh color
is worked.

Eyebrows: (Illustration 2 on Pull-out.)
With black floss, create arches of outward
slanting stitches. Make central stitches
close together for dense, fluffy brows and
those on the inner and outer edges
singular and not touching one another.
(For larger sizes, you may choose silver or
white with the black to create grey
brows.) Weave floss on back and clip tails
close to surface.

Brow Furrows, Nose, Cheeks, Mouth:
(Illustration 3 on Pull-out.) With rosy
pink floss make two rows of tiny back
stitches on the forehead for brow furrows.
Lock the first two stitches, and clip
thread ends close. Carry floss down at
back to right inner brow to outline nose
bridge in a vertical arching line. For
Santa's round nose. work tiny stitches
opposite each other traveling around in a
circle to create a 3 dimensional padded
ball. Use a few small back stitches for the
nostril outlines as illustrated. Carry
thread down at back from nose to work
lower lip. Here, the tinier the stitch, the
better his mouth will show up. Fill in the
inside of mouth with tiny red satin
stitches. Cheeks are worked in the same
manner as the nose in a circle of
opposing stitches for a padded "cheeky"
look. Smile creases are also worked in
pink under eyes and rest on rounded
cheeks. Weave floss back through and clip
ends.

Face: Before filling in Santa's face with

peachy flesh-toned floss, be sure that all black thread tails are clipped back to the surface on the back so none will show through. Begin either from each side of curl at forehead or the base of cheeks and make tiny stitches, following the contours of the face. Adjust the size of stitches to avoid excess bulk. For example, make the flesh colored stitches larger around the cheeks. Stitches from side to side should be tiny, however, to give a fleshy, warm appearance to the face.

Grey Swirls: For the swirls in the beard and the one on Santa's forehead, use small stitches so the grey will contrast with the white. Carry floss from one swirl in beard to the next, where possible.

Holly Leaves: On cuff and ball of cap and in the ribbon borders, the holly leaves are close satin stitches slanted outward from the center of each leaf, using longer stitches to create the sharp points. Sew on glass holly berries when entire design is completed.

Hat: Work white areas in the ball of the cap and around the face in small inner stitches and slightly larger outer ones. (You may piggy-back the stitches already worked if possible.) Complete the ice blue shaded portions of the ball and cap, taking larger stitches on the outer curve.

Glove: Backstitch the finger outlines excluding the outline of the hand. Beginning with the index finger, shadow stitch in small stitches down entire hand area. Work cuff in same manner as ball of cap, working the white ball behind the entire glove or working the white portion on each side of glove and holly leaves.

Beard and Mustache: For Santa's mustache, piggy-back tiny white stitches against those in the cheek, taking slightly larger stitches on the lower portion. Santa's beard is worked in sections as indicated on embroidery design.

Some of the swirls are used to separate the sections, in which case stitches may be piggy-backed. The white of the beard will be worked behind the swirls in the remaining sections.

Ribbon Borders: Satin stitch holly leaves, but do not add glass beads yet. For candy canes, work white satin stitches within alternating stripes and follow with red satin stitches on remaining stripes. For ribbon borders, take small stitches, remembering to use shorter stitches on the inner curves and slightly longer ones on outer curves.

Holly Berries: Sew tiny red glass beads in groups of three or more on the holly leaves on Santa's hat, cuffs and ribbon borders.

COLLAR CONSTRUCTION
To complete collar after design is worked, cut along outline. For neck, cut a strip of entredeux long enough to fit neck edge with at least 1" excess beyond each edge.

Press, starch and trim batiste edging from one side of entredeux. Cut lace edging approximately twice the length of the entredeux and gather by pulling a thread in the heading. Place gathered lace next to trimmed side of entredeux and zigzag together with needle going into each hole. Clip remaining edge of entredeux so that it will curve. Zigzag to neck edge, allowing edge of neck to roll over so that the needle swings from hole or edge of entredeux off fabric edge.

For outer edges of collar, cut entredeux to fit across bottom of front and backs, with some excess to allow for mitering. Trim batiste edge away. Do the same for sides and zigzag to edges by placing remaining $1/4$" edge of entredeux on the fabric edge, right sides together, and joining with a close medium-width zigzag. This method will allow the entredeux to show best. Cut lengths of beading, allowing excess for the front and back bottoms and sides. Press, starch and zigzag onto entredeux with a narrow stitch which goes into each hole. Use either a wide lace edging or insertion and edging zigzagged together. Allow at least $1 1/2$ to 2 times the length for each edge. Gather by pulling a thread in the heading and join to beading with medium-width zigzag. Miter edges on front and back corners and zigzag, cutting excess lace on underside.

Press under edges on back, fold under $3/4$" and either machine stitch or hem by hand. Using tear-away stabilizer or wax paper, make buttonholes on right back and sew buttons on left (beauty pins may be used instead). Run red or green ribbon through beading and tie bow in the back. To clean the finished collar, wash by hand in cool water using a mild detergent and press right side down on a thick terrycloth towel with a press cloth and moderate heat in areas where glass beads are sewn. ❧

Designed by Tina Lewis

This project requires much precision and patience. Because pieces are so small and maximum accuracy is needed, it is best to baste everything before machine stitching and to backstitch by hand, in some cases, instead of stitching by machine.

The purse is made of brown cotton velvet, but a variety of other fabrics may be used, such as wool, velveteen, heavy cotton, corduroy or felt.

Purchased appliqués, machine embroidery designs or hand embroidery designs may be used instead of some or all of the buttons.

All seams are $1/4$".

SUPPLIES
Gingerbread Purse Pattern on Pull-out
$1/4$ yd. brown fabric
1 yd. Pellon Craft Bond fusible
    interfacing
$1/4$ yd. each:
    red and white striped cotton
    green cotton with white pin dot
    red cotton with white pin dot

white cotton with tiny gold star print (solid white or white cotton with red pin dot can also be used)
1 yd. $1/4$" cording
23 red heart buttons
White baby rickrack
White embroidery floss
5 brown Velcro® $3/4$" dots
Assorted buttons for decoration: 8 poinsettias, 7 candy canes, 4 candles, 2 nutcracker, 2 wreaths, 2 gingerbread boys, 1 Santa, 1 elf, 1 rocking horse, 1 snowman, 1 tree, 1 angel and 1 tiny ball button for the doorknob.

INSTRUCTIONS
1. Cut and fuse the following pieces and set aside. Use a needle board or a piece of velvet if fusing to a napped fabric. Follow manufacturer's instructions for fusing.

Roof: Cut 2 of brown, 2 of green pin dot and 4 of interfacing. Fuse interfacing to wrong side of brown and green pieces.

Chimney: Cut 1 of brown, 1 of red pin dot and 1 of interfacing. Fuse interfacing to wrong side of brown piece.

House: Cut 2 brown and 2 interfacing. Fuse interfacing to the wrong side of both brown pieces.

Door: Cut 2 of red pin dot and 1 interfacing. Fuse interfacing to wrong side of 1 red piece.

Door Canopy: Cut 2 of green pin dot and 1 of interfacing. Fuse interfacing to wrong side of 1 green piece.

Shutters: Cut 8 of green pin dot (4 right side and 4 left side) and 4 interfacing. Fuse interfacing to wrong side of 4 green pieces (2 right side and 2 left side).

Windows: Cut a 5" x 5" square of white fabric and also of interfacing. Fuse interfacing to wrong side of fabric piece.

Mark fabric with crosshatch lines diagonally in a $1/2$" grid. Using a narrow dense satin stitch and red thread, stitch along all lines. Cut windows from completed stitched piece: 4 long windows, 2 side windows and 1 round window.

2. Make house. With right sides together, pin house to house facing. Stitch $1/4$" seams along straight top of each side and pointed top of front and back, leaving side seams open. Trim points at front and back. Turn right side out through a side opening. Press. On right side, chalk mark the stitching line around bottom of house. Topstitch along line, stitching house and facing pieces together. Then staystitch each side seam just inside the $1/4$" seamline, stitching house and facing together. Clip each inner corner (created by the side seams) to the corner of bottom stitching line as indicated on the pattern piece. Set aside.

3. Make candy cane pieces. Cut red and white striped fabric into bias strips $1 1/2$" wide. For the corner piping, cut 4 pieces of cording exactly $3 1/8$" long, wrapping cording in transparent tape at cutting points to prevent raveling. Cut 4 bias strips $4 1/8$" long. Press $1/2$" on ends of each bias strip. Enclose cording in bias strips. Baste; then stitch close to cording. Trim seam allowance to $1/4$". Set aside. For the handle, cover a 10" piece of cording with the bias by your favorite method. Cut to 9" long. Pull $1/4$" of cording out of each end and cut off so that thickness will be removed from the seam. Set handle aside.

4. Make shutters. With right sides together, pin the 4 interfaced shutter pieces to the shutter facing pieces. Stitch around edges in $1/4$" seam, leaving an opening where indicated on the pattern piece. Clip to dot. Trim corners and notch curves every $1/8$". Carefully turn

shutters right side out. Press. Using 6 strands of white floss, stab stitch $1/8$" stitches all around each shutter except for opening, stitching in $1/8$" in from edge. Set shutters aside.

5. Make door. Baste, then stitch a candy cane door piping piece to each side of door between dots. Slash door facing piece along indicated line. With right sides together, baste door to door facing. Stitch all around, stitching inside previous stitching at sides and being careful not to catch ends of cording. Trim corners and point. Turn right side out through slash. Press. Set door aside.

6. Make door canopy. Slash canopy facing along indicated line. Pin facing to door canopy, right sides together. Stitch $1/4$" seam all around. Trim corners and point. Notch curves every $1/8$" and clip at inner corner. Turn right side out through slash. Press. Using 6 strands of white floss, stab stitch $1/8$" all around, $1/8$" in from edge. Set door canopy aside.

7. Stitch windows. Place front and back windows into position on house as indicated on pattern piece. Baste in place. Using red thread, satin stitch all around windows. Then, using 6 strands of white floss, stab stitch $1/8$" stitches all around each window $1/8$" outside of red stitching. Pin side windows into position on each side of house. Slip a shutter in place on each side of the windows so that the shutter seam allowance is covered by window and the bottom of shutter is just above bottom of window. Baste in place, Using red thread, satin stitch all around side windows, catching in shutters. Using 6 strands of white floss, stab stitch $1/8$" stitches all around side windows $1/8$" outside of red stitching, except under shutters.

8. Assemble door. Center door on front of house between windows, having bottom of door $1/8$" above stitching line. Stitch door to house by hand or machine by stitching in the ditch between piping and door on each side. Center canopy above door so that it covers the top of piping. Pin in place, then slipstitch by hand along both sides of top, leaving free along lower edges of canopy.

9. Fold and stitch house. Place house wrong side up on ironing board and, one at a time, fold each side of the house back along bottom stitching line. Steam well along each folded edge so that a crease is formed all around bottom stitching line and house is shaped with walls perpendicular to bottom. Baste, then stitch, a corner candy cane piping piece to right side of one side seam in each corner. With right sides facing, bring seams together at each corner and baste. Stitch along each side seam just outside previous staystitching, catching in piping. Serge together (or zigzag) all seam allowances of each corner seam. Turn house right side out. Pinch the top of each house corner together above piping and, using brown thread, whip front or back to side securely at each corner, establishing a tight, square corner.

10. Sew buttons on house. Front: A nutcracker on each side of the door, a wreath on the door, a doorknob, a heart at the center of the door canopy, a candle in each long window, a poinsettia on each window sill, a Santa in the round window. Back: A candle in each window, a poinsettia on each window sill, an angel in the center of the wall and a tree between the windows along bottom. Sides: A heart on each shutter, a gingerbread boy in each window, 2 poinsettias on each window sill and a rocking horse and elf along bottom on one side and a snowman along bottom of other side.

11. Make roof. Baste, then stitch, rickrack to seamline of scalloped edges of both roof pieces, having only the peaks of the rickrack catching into the seam and making sure that the point of each scallop is between rickrack peaks. It is best to ease the rickrack rather than to stretch it. With right sides together, pin each roof piece to a green roof facing piece. Using a small stitch, follow the previous rickrack stitching and stitching around the scalloped edges, leaving straight edges open. Clip into scallop points and notch every $1/8$" around each scallop. Carefully turn each roof piece, shaping scallops by pulling out the rickrack peaks. Mark stitching grid on each roof piece with chalk. Using 6 strands of white floss, stab

stitch along grid marking with $1/8$" stitches. Then stab stitch all around scallops $1/8$" in from edge. Place each roof piece wrong side up on ironing board and fold scalloped edges back along fold lines indicated on pattern piece. Steam well to create a creased line around scalloped edges. Baste candy cane handle to one side of roof at points indicated along straight edge. With right sides of roof pieces together, baste and then stitch $1/4$" roof seam, catching in handle. Then serge (or zigzag) together the seam allowances of the roof seam, being careful not to catch in scallops or rickrack at each end.

12. Make chimney. Baste, then stitch rickrack to chimney along top seamline in the same way as rickrack was stitched to roof scallops. Staystitch along $1/4$" seamline of lower edge on chimney and chimney facing. Clip to staystitching the inner corners of both pieces, then press in seam allowances. With right sides together, pin chimney facing to chimney. Stitch top seam following previous rickrack stitching. Press seam toward facing. Now fold chimney lengthwise and stitch short side seam between dots. Press seam open. Turn right side out, then fold chimney facing down inside chimney and slipstitch bottom seamlines of chimney and facing together by hand all around. Crease and steam chimney along indicated corner foldlines and, using 6 strands of white floss, stab stitch $1/8$" stitches along edges of foldlines to hold creases in place and also along top of chimney. Place completed chimney on roof as indicated on pattern piece. Pin in place, then slipstitch securely by hand. Sew candy cane buttons to both sides of roof at indicated points where stitching crosses. Sew wreath button on chimney.

13. Sew roof to house. Place roof on house with chimney on the right side. Pin just the right side of roof to the house, having corner candy cane piping exactly between front and side scallops, the point of the front and back exactly at the roof seam (with point in front of seam) and making sure that the top edge of the front, side and back of house touch the foldline up under the scalloped edges. Pin or baste scallops in place. Using double thread, sew heart buttons in place

at points indicated on the pattern piece on each scallop. Sew through scallops and house so that roof is attached to the house. Then invisibly tack the first scallop in place on the front and the back starting at the point.

14. Finish. On the left (open) side of the roof, sew heart buttons to the scallops at the points indicated on the pattern piece. Cut Velcro® dots in half. By hand, stitch dot halves to the under side of each scallop and to exactly corresponding spots on the house, making sure that the left side of the roof fits in same manner as right side. 🍂

Gingerbread Dress *Shown on page 75*

Adapted by Tina Lewis

Dress and jacket are variations of "Just for Rosemary," by Becky B's. Smock plate is a variation of "Gingerbread Lane" by Lou Anne Lamar. Patterns available at fine needlework shops. See Resource Guide.

Dress is red Viyella®, or use any soft, draping light- to medium-weight fabric. Jacket (which matches "Gingerbread House") is cotton velvet. Wool, velveteen, heavy cotton, or corduroy may be substituted.

Trim and stitching treatments can be adapted to any jacket pattern. Cut a scalloped edge for the jacket, sleeves and collar, and trim with rickrack, contrasting top stitching, and red heart buttons. See "Gingerbread House" for suggestions on embellishments. 🍂

Designed by Tina Lewis

Dress is an adaptation of "Lily" by Children's Corner in green and black velvet. Pattern available at fine needlework shops. See Resource Guide.

The pictured dress features three tiers of pleated green taffeta, but velveteen, cotton, silk or other fabrics could be used. A variety of tree decorations could be used including ball buttons and beads. Many specialty threads could be used for the garland and more garlands could be added. Lights could be multicolored with added colors such as pink or purple or all white lights could be stitched with a white metallic thread. See template for

"Smocked Christmas Tree" on Pattern Pull-out.

Make tree taller or shorter to fit size of garment. Tree top should be 3" below center front neckline. Lower edge of tree curves $1/2$" below lower edge of top at center front. Lower corners of tree touch lower edge of top on each side. Alter the width of each tree tier if tree is made taller or shorter.

1. Cut 3 pieces of green taffeta.
   Top: 4" x $5^1/2$"
   Center: $4^3/4$ x 13"
   Lower: $5^1/4$" x 23"

2. In matching thread, serge one long edge of each tier. Turn under opposite long edge 1" and press. Turn each remaining short edge under $1/2$" and press.

3. Roll each piece through a pleater, pleat using transfer dots, or have fabric pleated by a smocking specialty shop (see Resource Guide). Make sure that first pleated row is $1/2$" in from long folded edge. Folded edge will become the ruffle at bottom of each tier.

4. Draw threads to back of each tier on both sides. Knot each thread along one side and draw up each tier so that it conforms to the tree template. (See Template on Pull-out.) Knot threads, draw up top tier very tightly at top so that it is $1/2$" wide and whip pleats together securely.

5. Backsmock every row of each tier

snugly with an outline stitch.

6. Turn to right side and, starting at lower left of each tier, outline stitch using one strand of gold metallic ribbon floss, curving up 2 rows to the right side. Turn work and repeat, stitching another swag of the garland. Complete garland on all three tiers.

7. Remove guide threads, except for top row of each tier.

8. Add lights if desired. To make light sockets, use Kreinik black braid and stitch over two pleats, approximately 6 pleats apart, alternating on each side of garland. Light bulbs are 2 strands of ribbon floss in small pistil stitches.

9. Decorate tree tiers with scattered buttons and star charms.

10. Using chalk or basting thread, outline tree template onto finished bodice front.

11. Position finished lower tree tier on bodice and slipstitch in place. Position center tier so that it covers $1/4$" of lower tier and slipstitch. Position top tier $1/4$" over center tier and slipstitch, making sure that tree top is as small as possible.

12. Add a star button at the top, covering top of tree. Gift and toy buttons may be added at each side of the tree at the lower edge. ❧

Designed by Tina Lewis

SUSPENDER TABS & BLOUSE

Use any commercial pattern for basic pants and button-front blouse.

Suspenders can be added to most commercial pants or skirt patterns.

Blouse fabric pictured was created by zigzagging together hemstitched handkerchiefs to form sufficient fabric for each pattern piece. Plan carefully for placement of hemstitching. Shadow work holly leaves and berries were embroidered at handkerchief intersections and collar edges.

A similar result can be achieved by machine hemstitching a purchased blouse or any basic blouse pattern. Weave 6 strands of floss through openings of hemstitching. Add shadow work embroidery design (on Pattern Pull-out). See "Shadow Work Basics" for embroidery instructions.

SUSPENDER TABS

1. From 12" x 12" square of green Ultrasuede®, cut 4 suspender tabs (see Pattern Pull-Out). From Wonder Under®, cut 2 suspender tabs.

2. Fuse Wonder Under® to the wrong side of 2 tabs. Peel paper. Fuse to wrong side of 2 remaining tabs.

3. Using green rayon machine embroidery thread, edgestitch all around each tab; work machine buttonholes at each end of tabs. Stitch center veins from buttonholes to points.

4. Fold each tab in half lengthwise and edgestitch between points indicated over first stitching.

5. Position red "berry" buttons on waistband approximately 2" apart. Button on tabs having smaller leaf towards center. Additional buttons may be stitched to the tabs to create berry clusters. ❧

Designed by Tina Lewis

MATERIALS

DMC Floss:
Blanc neige–snow, horizon
Red 817–sleigh, rider's cap, cat's collar
Green 986–trees
Golden brown 780–window frame
Gold 782–house window light
Flesh 3778–rider's face
Blue 798–rider's jacket
Tan 840–horse
Black 310–eye of horse
Light gray 318–moon
Brown 801–horse whip, horse hooves,
    tail and mane, harness
Gray 317–Sleigh runners, horse

Patchwork sleigh quilt is one stitch each
of 986, 317, 550, 920, 782, 3685, 831,
890, 924.

This design covers 184 pleats. Stitch with
4 strands of floss unless otherwise noted.
Backsmock Rows 2-8 and Rows 10-16.

Stitch entire window frame. For
horizontal lines, cable 2 rows each across
Rows 1, 9 and 17, starting the top row of
each with an up cable and the second row
with a down cable. Fill in half-stitches at

ends. For vertical
lines, satin stitch
over groups of 4
pleats so that
spacing is 4-56-4-
56-4-56-4.

Complete snow in
each windowsill.
Fill in half stitches
along the sides.

Stitch falling snow
in upper center
and upper right
windows, working
vertically. Each
snowflake covers 2
pleats with one
row between
snowflakes vertically, four pleats between
snowflakes horizontally, and three pleats
along each side of window. Each vertical
line of snowflakes alternates the next by
$1/2$ row.

Stitch moon in upper left window with
starting stitch on Row 5, 16 pleats from
left side of window. Complete falling
snow in upper left window.

Stitch large trees on right and left sides of
lower windows. Fill in half-stitches along
sides of trees.

Stitch horizon line along all lower
windows using an outline stitch and 3
strands.

Complete stacking in lower windows.
Extra stitches may need to be added at
the base of the houses and little trees so
that they connect with the horizon line.

Lower left window: Begin large tree on
Row 14, first pleat from left side of
window.

Begin house on Row 11, 17 pleats from

left side of window.
Begin horse on Row 13, 25 pleats from
right side of window.

Chimney smoke is straight stitches using
1 strand.

Horse ears are straight stitches. Horse eye
is 2 strand French knot. Harness is
straight stitch using 3 strands.

Fill in falling snow after stacking is
complete.

Lower center window: Begin tree on Row
$10^1/2$, 21 pleats from the right side of
window.

Begin sleigh on Row 13, 11 pleats from
left side of window. Patchwork sleigh
quilt is one stitch of each of the nine
colors listed. Order of colors:

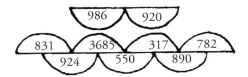

Quilt can also be stitched in a solid color.
Gold 831 or gray 317 are suggested.

Whip handle is a 1-strand, 30-wrap
bullion over 7 pleats. Whip is outline
stitch using 1 strand of floss. Harness is a
3-strand straight stitch.

Sleigh runner is outline stitch along Row
14 using 3 strands and curving up at
front. Sleigh runner covers pleats 4
through 37, counting from left side of
window.

Vertical runner attachments are satin
stitched over one pleat using 3 strands.

Fill in falling snow after stacking is
complete.

Lower right window: Begin house on

Row 11, 20 pleats from the right side of window.

Begin tree on Row 13, 10 pleats from right side of window.

Chimney smoke is straight stitches using 1 strand.

Fill in falling snow after stacking is complete.

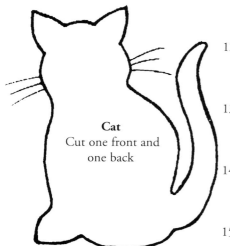

Cat
Cut one front and one back

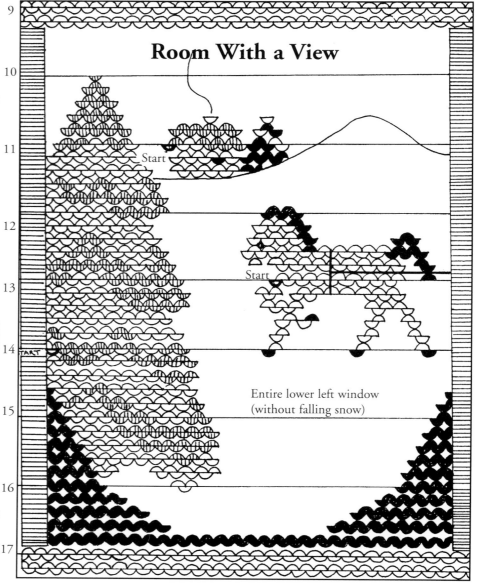

Room With a View

Start

Start

Entire lower left window (without falling snow)

From cat pattern, cut one front and one back of Ultrasuede®. Place wrong sides together and hand whip edges together all around with tiny stitches using one strand of matching floss. Lightly stuff the tail and body as they are enclosed. Collar is a crocheted chain, using 6 strands of floss. A tiny bell can be attached to the collar, if desired. Whiskers are single strands of floss sewn through from one side of head to the other, then stiffened with a touch of Fray Check® and trimmed when dry. Completed cat is tacked in placed invisibly from the back along the center of body. A jewelry pin or hook and loop pieces could also be used to make the cat removable.

Notes: In addition to its use on garments, this design could be charming on the bib of an apron or the padded cover of an album or as a framed piece. It would make a lovely decorative pillow or could be used as the centerpiece of a larger pillow.

Create a daytime version of this design by using lighter blue, blue-gray or gray fabric. Substitute a full-circle yellow

(DMC 725) sun instead of the moon.

White fabric can be successfully used by stitching the snow in a very pale blue (DMC 3756). For sparkle, a strand or two of Kreinik blending filament can be added to the moon and/or the snow.

The window sizes can easily be altered to complement the design of a garment. Or, all of the elements in the six windows could be repositioned in just four windows for a smaller size bib front. ❧

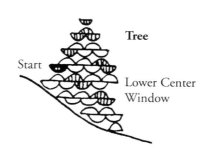

Tree
Start
Lower Center Window

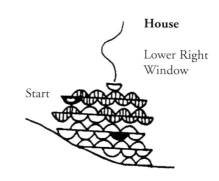

House
Lower Right Window
Start

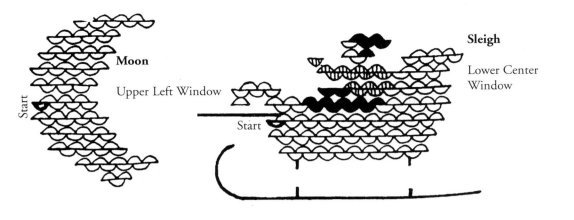

Moon

Upper Left Window

Start

Sleigh

Lower Center Window

Start

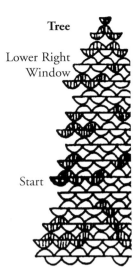

Tree

Lower Right Window

Start

Shown on pages 80 & 81 *Christmas Candy*

Designed by Tina Lewis

Dress is a variation of "The Bow Dress" by The Smocking Horse Collection in silk doupioni with gold braid or piping. Pattern available at fine needlework shops. See Resource Guide.

INSTRUCTIONS

This design covers 178 pleats and 21 rows. Backsmock every row. *Note: The silk doupioni dress shown was backed with batiste before it was pleated to create fuller pleats. Follow graph for stitching and vertical spacing.*

PEPPERMINT STICK
Threads:
  White Ribbon Floss® – 1 strand
  Red Ribbon Floss® – 1 strand
  Green rayon machine embroidery
    thread – 2 strands

Peppermint stick is 3 rows of cable stitches alternating 6 red cables with 8 white cables across each row. To begin on the left side, cable 4 in red on the bottom row, beginning with a down cable on the first pleat. Cable 5 on the middle row beginning with an up cable on the first pleat and cable 6 on the top row, beginning with a down cable on the first pleat. Green stripes are 3 long straight stitches, diagonally across each white section.

LEMON DROPS
Threads:
  DMC 104 (variegated yellow) and
  Kreinik blending filament
    032 – 3 strands each

Spacing: 9 lemon drops in the row, each covering 16 pleats with 4 pleats between them and 1 pleat at each end of row.

FOIL-WRAPPED HARD CANDY
Threads:
  Each candy in the two rows of hard

candies is stitched with 1 strand of a different thread including Ribbon Floss® in purple, fuchsia and copper and Kreinik 1/16" ribbons in colors 127, 1800, 045, 095, 044, 041 and 2829.

Spacing: 5 candies in the row, each covering 26 pleats with 8 pleats between them, and 8 pleats at each end of row.

KISSES
Threads:
  Silver Metallic Ribbon Floss® – 1
    strand

Spacing: 9 kisses in the row, each covering 14 pleats with 6 pleats between them and 2 pleats at each end of the row.

PEPPERMINTS
Threads:
  Opal Metallic Ribbon Floss® – 1
    strand (cellophane)
  Red Ribbon Floss® – 1 strand

Spacing: 7 peppermints in the row, each covering 22 pleats with 4 pleats between them and no pleats at each end of row.

Red swirls are 2 straight stitches from center to the outside edges that are tacked at their midpoint with red rayon

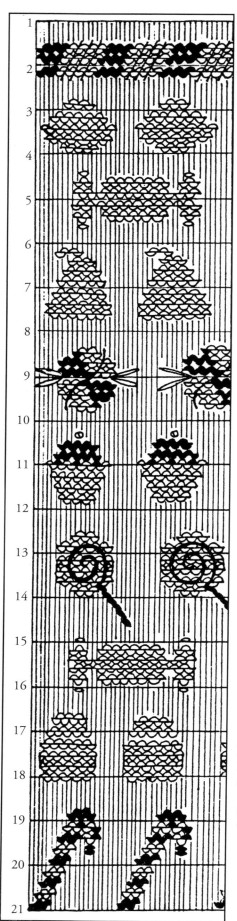

machine embroidery thread into a slight curve. Cellophane ends are 2 straight stitches covering 6 pleats.

CHOCOLATES IN FOIL CUPS
Threads:
  Red Ribbon Floss® – 1 strand (sprinkle)
  Brown Ribbon Floss® – 1 strand (chocolate)
  Gold Metallic Ribbon Floss® – 1 strand (cup)

Spacing: 9 cups in the row, each covering 14 pleats with 6 pleats between them and 2 pleats at each end of the row. Sprinkle is a French knot.

LOLLIPOPS
Threads:
  Purple Ribbon Floss® – 1 strand (grape)
  Lemon yellow Ribbon Floss® – 1 strand (lemon)
  Berry pink Ribbon Floss® – 1 strand (berry)
  Orange Ribbon Floss® – 1 strand (orange)
  Cinnamon beige Ribbon Floss® – 1 strand (sticks)
  White Ribbon Floss® – 1 strand (swirls)

Spacing: 8 lollipops in the row, each covering 16 pleats with 6 pleats between them and 5 pleats at the left end of the row and 3 pleats at the right end of the row.

Swirls are 1 strand of white brought up just above the stick and couched down in a swirl using a separate needle threaded with 1 strand of white rayon machine embroidery thread. The Ribbon Floss® is inserted back through at the center. Sticks are 6 trellis stitches.

FOIL-WRAPPED HARD CANDY
Repeat previous hard candy row using a different assortment of metallic threads.

SUGAR PLUMS
Threads:
  DMC 347, Kreinik blending filament 032 (3 strands each); Rainbow blending thread 612 pink (2 strands) – Cherry
  DMC 727, Rainbow blending thread

403 yellow (3 strands each) – Lemon
Kreinik fine braid 9192 (1 strand) and DMC 971 (2 strands) – Orange
DMC 210 and Kreinik blending filament 093 (3 strands each) – Grape
Kreinik $1/16$" ribbon 9194 and DMC 701(1 strand each) – Lime

Spacing: 10 sugar plums in the row, each covering 12 pleats, with 6 pleats between them and 2 pleats at each end of the row.

CANDY CANES
Threads:
  Red Ribbon Floss® – 1 strand
  White Ribbon Floss® – 1 strand

Spacing: 9 candy canes in the row, each covering 15 pleats with 4 pleats between them and no pleats at the left end of the row and 3 pleats at the right end of the row. ❧

Thread kit for "Candy Dress" smock design available from Miss Maureen's. See Resource Guide.

Designed by Pat Ferebee

Baby bubble is a variation of "Ashley" by Children's Corner in 100% cotton silky broadcloth with pearl buttons and eyelet trim.

Dress is Chery Williams' "Basic Square Yoke Dress" in 100% cotton silky broadcloth with gathered embroidered wide edging for collar. Both patterns available at fine needlework shops. See Resource Guide.

INSTRUCTIONS FOR "MERRY BERRY" SHOWN ON DRESS
DMC Floss:
Green 911
Red beads for berries

Design covers 146 pleats.

1. Pleat number of rows recommended in pattern instructions.

2. With steam iron, block the pleated piece to fit yoke guide. Mark center.

3. Using floss the same color as fabric, backsmock entire yoke area with diamonds made from one-step waves. Do

not remove pleating threads until entire yoke is smocked.

4. Using four strands of floss, work three motifs.

5. Smock holly leaves placing the lower smocking rows of the middle motif on the next to the last pleated row.

6. The lower smocking rows of the outside motifs should be placed on the fifth pleated row from the bottom.

7. When smocking is complete, center and pin paper yoke guide over entire smocked area. Remove paper guide and pleating threads. Trim just outside machine stitching.

8. Assemble dress according to pattern instructions.

VARIATION FOR "MERRY BERRY" SHOWN ON BUBBLE

DMC Floss:
Green 911
Red beads for berries
1. Pleat fabric according to pattern

instructions.

2. With steam iron, block pleated piece. Mark center.

3. Using floss the same color as fabric, backsmock all rows with diamonds made from one-step waves.

4. Stitch a half-row 2-step trellis between Rows 1 and $1^1/_2$ and 5 and $5^1/_2$.

5. For front panels of bubble, stitch two holly leaves with one set of berries in center of panel. For back of bubble, stitch entire graph, omitting center holly berries. Using graph as a guide, smock holly leaves with four strands of floss.

6. When smocking is complete, add red beads for berries. ❧

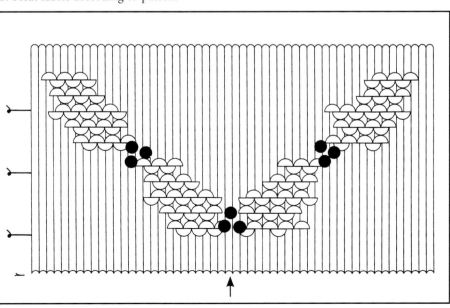

Designed by Chery Williams

Nightgown is an adaptation of "Bishops and Bonnets" by Chery Williams in cotton flannel. Pattern available at fine needlework shops. See Resource Guide.

INSTRUCTIONS
DMC Floss
Red 321
Green 909

Backsmock Rows 3 and 5. "Noel" covers 76 pleats. Mark center pleat. Entire design is worked with 3 strands, unless otherwise indicated.

Work cable on Row 1, beginning with a down cable. Work baby wave diamond directly below. Start baby wave with level stitch halfway between Rows 1 and 2, and work up to cable. Start second baby wave directly below first and work down to Row 2.

Center design begins on Row 4. Work 3 cable stitches, first stitch down, then a four-step wave up (each step $1/4$ space). At Row 3 work 7 cables, then a 4-step wave down (each step $1/4$ space). Repeat 3 times, ending with 3 cables, last stitch down. Work mirror image for bottom half of design.

Letters are worked with 2 strands, spaced between Row $3^1/2$ and $4^1/2$. Satin stitch over 2 pleats for vertical lines. Horizontal lines are outline stitch with thread above the needle. The diagonal line in the "N" is a 5-step wave.

Flower design is composed of 3 French knots, using 2 strands and 3 wraps. The leaves are lazy daisy stitches, using 2 strands. &

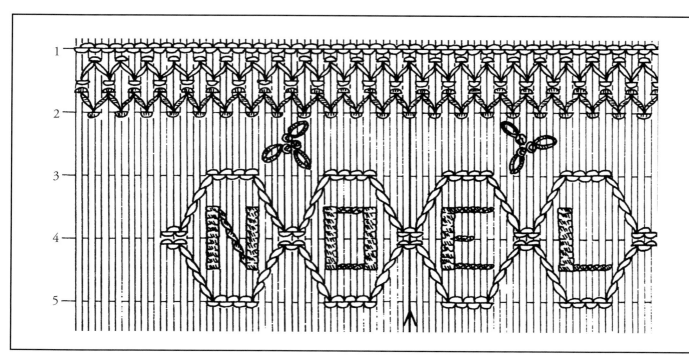

Designed by Chris DeMars Victorsen

Dress is a variation of "Basic Yoke Dress" by Chery Williams. Pattern available at fine needlework shops. See Resource Guide.

INSTRUCTIONS

DMC Floss:

Red 304	Green 699
Flesh 754	Gray 415
Gold 725	Pink 3326
Black 310	Blanc neige

All floss should be stripped; 4 strands are used throughout.

Each Santa covers 76 pleats. Two Santa stars will fit on 45 inches of pleated fabric.

1. Backsmock Rows 2 through 11 with one strand of #8 perle cotton or 2 strands of floss.

2. Using the floss the same color as fabric, cable across Rows 1 and 12. (The cable row may be stitched on the back of fabric.)

3. For right Santa, count 7 pleats to the right of center on Row 5. Beginning with an up cable, cable across Row 5, changing color as indicated by the smocking graph. Turn and complete lower part of star, increasing, decreasing and changing colors as indicated by the graph.

4. Work head as indicated by graph.

5. To work second Santa, count 7 pleats to left of center. Turning fabric upside down and beginning with a down cable, cable across Row 5, changing colors as indicated by the graph. Continue with steps 3 and 4.

6. Mustache is made with four strands of white worked in two straight stitches as shown on graph. Finish belt buckle with two straight stitches, using four strands of gold floss. These stitches should be made so that end stitches of both rows of gold cables are covered by straight stitches.

(Refer to picture for exact placement)

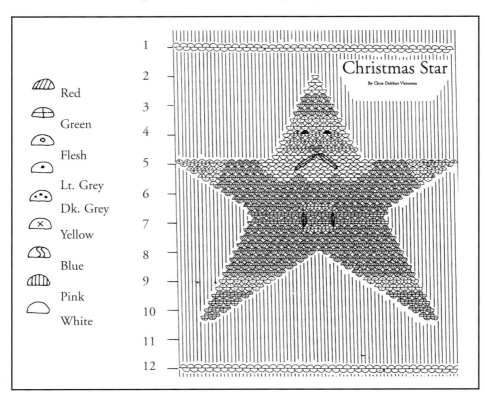

Red

Green

Flesh

Lt. Grey

Dk. Grey

Yellow

Blue

Pink

White

Christmas Star
By Chris DeMars Victorsen

Winter Star *Shown on page 85*

Designed by Chris DeMars Victorsen

"Winter Star," a variation of "Christmas Star," is a season-long design, usable all through the winter.

INSTRUCTIONS

DMC Floss:

Blanc Neige	Red 304
Yellow 726	Blue 797
Green 909	Black 310
Orange 722	

All floss should be stripped; 4 strands are used throughout unless otherwise noted.

Each snowman covers 76 pleats. Two snowmen will fit on 45 inches of pleated fabric.

1. Backsmock Rows 2 through 11 with one strand of #8 perle cotton or 2 strands of floss.

2. Using floss the same color as fabric, cable across Rows 1 and 12. (This cable row may be stitched on the back of fabric.)

3. For right snowman, count 7 pleats to the right of center on Row 5. Beginning with an up cable, cable across Row 5, changing colors as shown on the graph. Turn and continue to work bottom of star, increasing, decreasing and changing colors as shown on graph.

4. Work head as indicated on graph.

5. To work second snowman, count 7 pleats to the left of center. Turning fabric upside down and beginning with a down cable, cable across Row 5, changing colors as shown on graph. Continue with steps 3 and 4.

6. Scarf fringe is 5 straight stitches worked with 2 strands of red. Eyes and buttons are 6-strand 1-wrap French knots. Mouth is four 4-strand 1-wrap French knots. The holly on hat is 2 lazy daisy stitches using 4 strands of green. Holly berry is one 4-strand 1-wrap French knot. The carrot nose is a 4-strand 8-wrap bullion stitch using orange floss. ❧

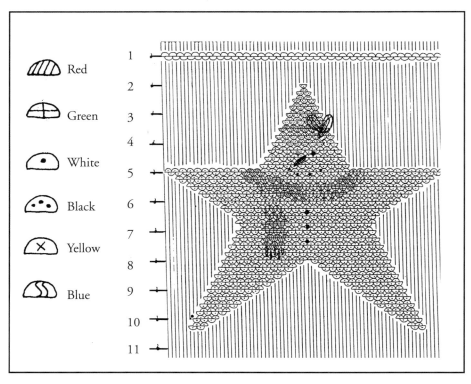

Designed by Trudy Horne with embellishments by Tina Lewis

Shortall is "Sunset and Overall Set" by Mollie Jane Taylor in 100% cotton corduroy. Shirt is "Small Stuff for Boys" by Angel Wears in cotton broadcloth. Smocked border is "Toy Soldiers" by Mollie Jane Taylor. Patterns available in fine needlework shops. See Resource Guide.

INSTRUCTIONS

DMC Floss:

Green 910	Red 321
Gold 727	Blue 798
Flesh 948	Grey 414
Black	White

Each nutcracker is worked over 20 pleats using 4 strands of floss. Middle figure is centered on pleated piece with remaining two placed at equidistant intervals.

Begin on Row 5 by working 11 cables in red. See arrow on graph. Turn and continue working remainder of red coat up to Row 3. Next work head, hat, sleeves, gloves, pants and boots, using graph and legend as guide. Fill in sides of head, sleeves and hat with half stitches as indicated on graph.

Backsmock between Rows 1 and 7. Geometric or figured borders may be added above or below nutcrackers.

ACCENTS AND EMBELLISHMENTS

Beard and hair are turkey work, using one or two strands of white or grey floss. See illustrations for turkey work. Moustache, pants divider, and hat accent are worked with straight stitches, using two strands of black; eyes are French knots using two or three strands of blue.

Stripes on coat are worked with two strands of gold floss. Small gold beads are sewn on boot tops, sleeves, top of hat, and at each end of stripes.

Turkey Work

Use two strands of floss doubled over and #11 or #12 sharp needle.

To begin, insert needle in fabric as illustrated, leaving a 1" tail.

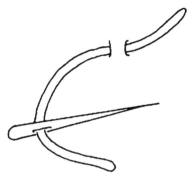

Illustration 1

Take a small stitch (go in same holes), holding tail with left thumb and locking stitch by pulling tightly.

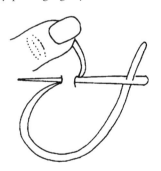

Illustration 2

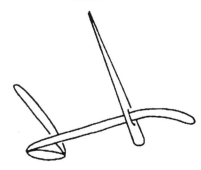

Illustration 3

Take another stitch to the right of first stitch, holding loop of thread above needle.

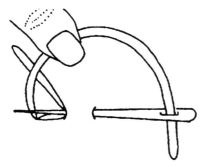

Illustration 4

Take a small stitch (go in same holes), locking stitch by pulling tightly.

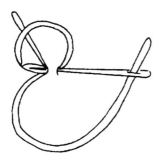

Illustration 5

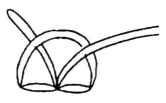

Illustration 6

Continue working from left to right, looping and locking, looping and locking.

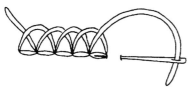

Illustration 7

Remember: thread above to loop; thread below to lock. Closely align rows of turkey work to produce a full fringe.

Turkey work may be clipped or not. If loops are not cut, then each one should be approximately the same size. ❧

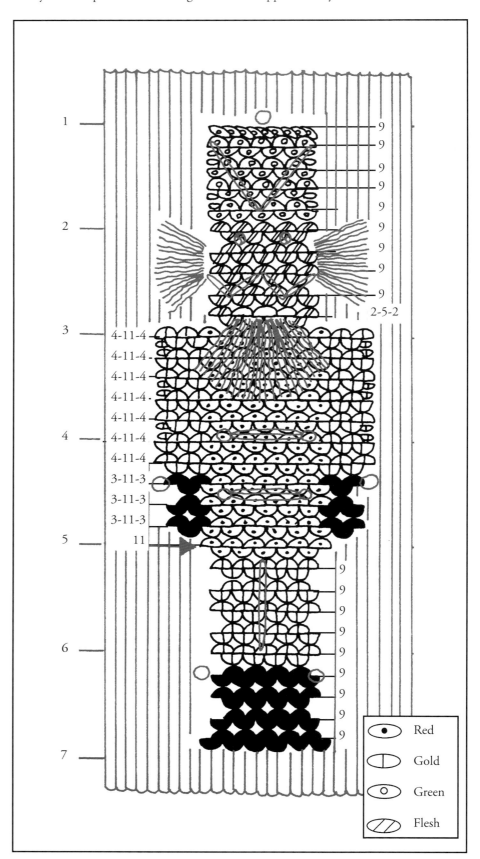

Designed by Tina Lewis

Pinafore is a variation of "Annie's Apron" by Becky B's, in cotton Swiss broderie anglaise, shown on a basic long-sleeved green velvet dress. Smocked panel is medium-weight cotton. Pinafore is edged with gingham bias binding. Pattern available at fine needlework shops. See Resource Guide.

INSTRUCTIONS
DMC Floss:
Red 321 – bow, holly berries
Dk. green 890 – large holly leaves, garland holly sprigs
Lt. green 320 – garland base, large holly leaf veins

This design requires 148 pleats for bow, but can be a total of any even number of pleats in excess of 148.

Note: This design can cover more than 11 rows simply by making more space between the bow and the borders. Center the bow and stitch the borders farther out from center, with equal distances at top and bottom.

In pictured pinafore, "Holly Bow" design is slightly adapted. The border garlands are curved in from center width to follow the contour of the waistband. Waistband is bound close to the borders so that at its center, the smocking is 9 rows wide. At the sides, it curves down to 7 rows wide.

Borders: Use 4 strands for garland, 3 strands for holly sprigs and 3 strands for holly berries. Begin at center of third row. Outline stitch across 2, then up 7 to the second row, across 4, then back down 7 to the third row, across 4, then up 7 again to the second row. Continue across the width of the piece. Turn work and repeat, completing the garland to the opposite side. Holly sprigs are 3 straight stitches at either side of the midpoint of each diagonal. Holly berries are French knots at the center of the holly sprigs along the garland and scattered at both sides of the garland. Repeat the garland between Rows 9 and 10.

Holly: Use 4 strands for holly and 1 strand for veins. Holly berries are six strand French knots. Follow graph. Begin at the indicated black stitch on Row 7 at the 19th pleat to right of center. Work veins down center of the completed leaves in backstitch. Add a few branch veins with straight stitches. Finish holly by stitching 5 berries as shown. Repeat for

holly leaves to the left side by turning work and beginning at the indicated black stitch on Row 5 at the 19th pleat to right of center.

Bow: Use 4 strands. The bow combines satin stitch over 2 pleats with wheat stitch (outline stitch next to stem stitch). Complete satin stitch segments. For upper bow loop, begin on Row 6 at center. Satin stitch over 2 pleats up to Row 4. On Row 4 at 17th pleat to left of center, satin stitch over 2 pleats down $^3/_4$ of the way to Row 5. For lower bow loop, begin on Row 6 at second pleat to left of center. Satin stitch over 2 pleats, down to Row 8. On Row 8 at 16th pleat to right of center, satin stitch over 2 pleats up $^3/_4$ of the way to Row 5.

Connect satin stitch segments with wheat stitch by completing outer curve of bow loops as shown on graph and the small segment of satin stitch diagonally back to center.

To obtain accurate stitches, draw bow loops and bow ends directly on pleats with an air soluble marker or light pencil marks.

Stitch bow ends with wheat stitch following graph. Stitch over 4 pleats at center of bow several times, drawing stitches together and covering intersections of all stitches, creating the knot at center of bow. (See following page for graph.) ❦

1

2

3

4

5

6

7

8

9

10

11

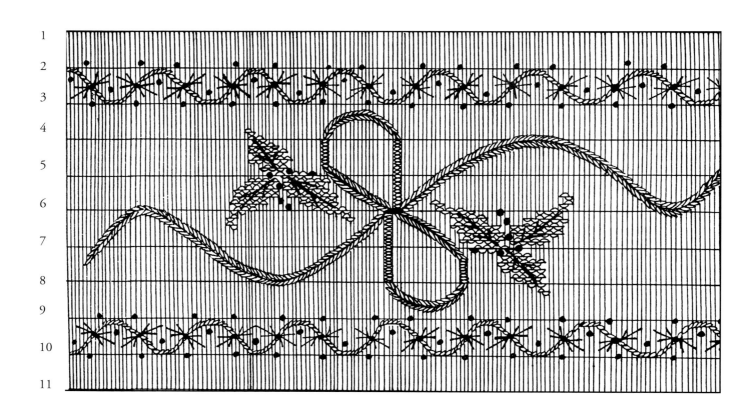

The Definition of Shadow Work

Two rows of stitches are worked on transparent fabric. The criss-crossed threads on the wrong side of the fabric produce the "shadow" which appears on the right side.

Suitable Fabrics for Shadow Work

Use 100% cotton batiste, organdy, lawn or sheer linen.

Thread and Needle Sizes

Use one strand of 6-strand embroidery floss or floche and a #10 crewel, a #7 between or #26 tapestry needle.

The Technique

Shadow work is worked on the wrong side of the fabric using the closed herringbone stitch. The result on the right side is two rows of backstitch with a shadow between them. To trace embroidery design onto fabric, place fabric (wrong side up) over design. Pin in place and trace design with a soft graphite pencil.

The secret to perfect shadow work is the precise and calculated execution of tiny stitches which should pick up no more than 1/8" of fabric.

In shadow work, the needle comes out through the same hole produced by a previous stitch, except for the first stitch.

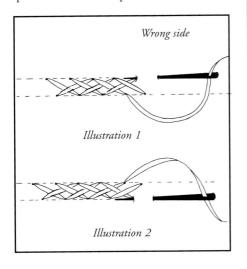

Wrong side

Illustration 1

Illustration 2

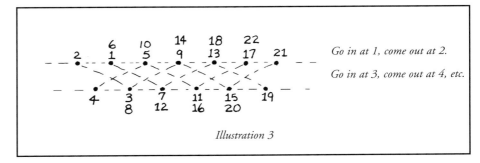

Go in at 1, come out at 2.

Go in at 3, come out at 4, etc.

Illustration 3

Note that the two rows of backstitch are positioned in a brick-like manner, and are not placed one on top of the other.

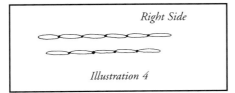

Right Side

Illustration 4

Working a Curve

The stitches on the outside of a curve will be longer and stitches on the inside of a curve will be shorter.

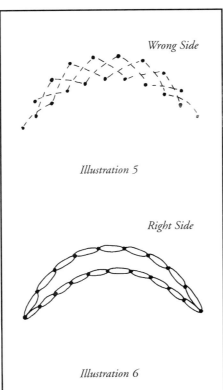

Wrong Side

Illustration 5

Right Side

Illustration 6

Working a Circle

To execute shadow work embroidery in a circle (or related shape) begin with a few outline stitches, then expand into the closed herringbone.

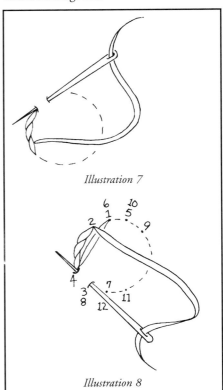

Illustration 7

Illustration 8

Working Changing Shapes

Many shadow work motifs are contoured, often changing widths and narrowing to a single line. To solve this problem, work an outline stitch along the single line, then expand to the closed herringbone as the motif widens.

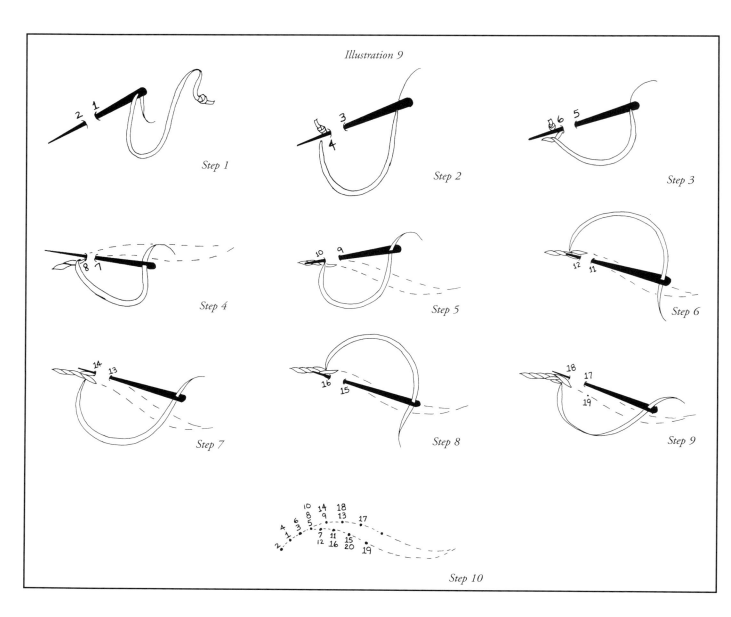

Illustration 9

Step 1

Step 2

Step 3

Step 4

Step 5

Step 6

Step 7

Step 8

Step 9

Step 10

Starting and Ending

Use one of these methods: Use regular knots (as in Step 1 in Illustration 9). At the end of the thread, tie off with any knot that lies close to the fabric.

Use waste knots and tuck stitches. To begin, knot one end of thread and anchor knot to fabric about 4" away from the placement of first stitch. This is called a waste knot.

Work the embroidery until you have about 4" of thread remaining.

Still working on the wrong side, take a small stitch behind each backstitch along one side only. These stitches are "tucked" underneath the surface stitches and concealed.

Cut away waste knot, thread needle and work tuck stitches as above. 🐾

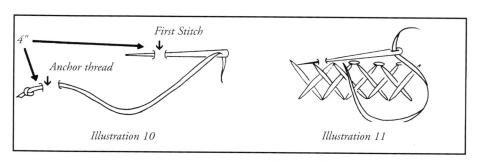

Illustration 10

Illustration 11

PLEATING THE FABRIC

Use a pleater, a pleating service (available at fine needlework stores) or transfer dots To use transfer dots: Test iron-on dots on scrap of fabric for washability. Cut transfer sheet to size needed (width of fabric x number of required rows plus two). Place transfer dots on wrong side of fabric with the parallel rows of dots on the crosswise grain. Iron according to transfer instructions.

Cut a piece of quilting thread for each row of dots. Thread length should be the width of fabric plus 6". Thread needle. Pick up each dot by pushing the needle in the right side of dot and out to the left side of the same dot. Pick up dots from right to left, keeping needle parallel to dot row. After all rows are threaded, carefully pull the threads to gather fabric and form pleats. Smock on the right side of fabric.

CABLE STITCH

The cable is a smocking stitch that does not have much elasticity. Cable rows may be used for stability in the neck borders of bishop yoke dresses and round collars, but never for the flared portion of lower bishop borders.

Notice the terms *gathering thread, pleat and valley*. These terms are seen often on smocking instructions.

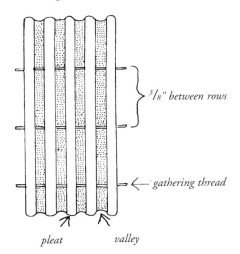

3/8" between rows

gathering thread

pleat   valley

Pull floss from skein and cut a length about 18". To keep strands from twisting while stitching, strip floss by separating each strand into individual pieces, and reassemble the number of strands required for design. Thread freshly cut end of floss into needle.

Knot the end of the floss and begin stitch, as shown in Step 1, stitching through Step 5 and continuing across for the required number of cables. Stitch horizontally, left to right, keeping the needle parallel to the gathering threads. Do not stitch exactly over a gathering thread. Choose either to stitch just above or just below thread. If stitching above, for example, continue to stitch above. Do not alternate above and below gathering thread for the up and down cables. If a gathering thread is snagged while smocking, remove the stitch. The caught thread will cause problems when blocking finished panel.

Step 1

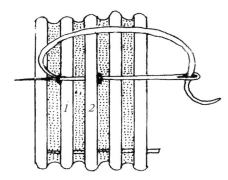

First Cable

Bring needle out of left side of pleat #1 about 2/3 to 3/4 of pleat depth. Bring needle over and enter fabric at right side of pleat #2; stitch through pleat #2.

Step 2

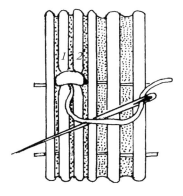

First cable is completed by pulling downward on floss. Do not pull too tightly.

Step 3

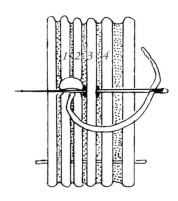

Second Cable
Insert needle in right side of pleat #3 and stitch through pleat.

Step 4

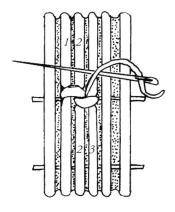

Second cable is completed by pulling upward on floss. Do not pull too tightly.

Step 5

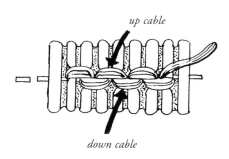

The needle will travel through each pleat, forming a cable.

The cable stitch may be smocked with two, three or four strands of floss. Individual design plates give instructions as to the recommended number of strands. Each strand of floss should lay parallel to the other strands on each cable for perfect stitching.

up cable

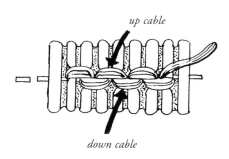

down cable

Each cable is either an "up" cable or a "down" cable, and will fall alternately above and below gathering rows. When stitching a "down" cable, the floss will be up as illustrated in Step 4. When stitching an "up" cable, the floss will be down as in Step 2.

Backsmocking is used to hold unsmocked pleats that cover over $1^1/2$ gathering rows in place. Unless another stitch is specified, stitch a continuous cable row, using two strands of floss in a color matching the fabric.

Flowerettes are accent stitches formed with cables. Two different stitches are illustrated here.

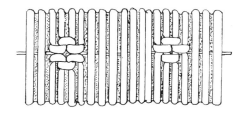

The six-cable flowerette is smocked by stitching two groups of three cables each, meeting at the horizontal center.

The four-cable flowerette is a three-cable group stitched with a single cable centered just below.

"Tie off" is a term which means ending one portion of smocking before beginning another.

When at the end of a smocking row or when at the end of a piece of floss, secure the free end by one of the following methods.

Begin each method by inserting the needle in the valley between the last two stitches smocked and pulling it through to the back side.

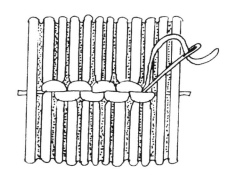

Smock three or four stitches to secure the floss. Always stitch back in the same direction from which you have just smocked.

Knotting the thread is another tie-off method. Turn fabric over to the back side and stitch through top $1/3$ of a pleat under

the portion just smocked. Wrap the floss two or three times around the needle. Pull needle through the fabric until the needle is pulled free.

Continue pulling the floss until a knot is formed where the floss exits the fabric. Tighten with your fingers. Clip thread ends no shorter than $1/4$".

OUTLINE STITCH

The outline stitch and the stem stitch, generally smocked in straight rows, are used in geometric designs and in the borders of picture smocking, but not in places where elasticity is required.

The outline stitch is smocked from left to right. The thread will ALWAYS be held above the needle. Each individual stitch will slant obliquely from lower left to upper right, making an "S" curve. Do not slant the needle! The needle will always be held parallel to gathering threads.

Step 1

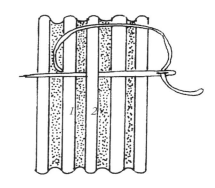

Begin stitching by bringing the needle out of the left side of pleat #1 about $2/3$ to $3/4$ of the pleat depth. Enter fabric at the right side of pleat #2—stitch through pleat #2.

Step 2

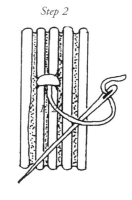

Pull floss downward after the first (and each) stitch. Initially, the first stitch will not lay obliquely. It will angle after the next stitch or two are in place.

Step 3

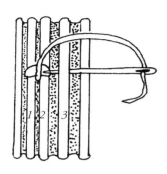

Take the floss to the "above the needle" position. Smock the next stitch by inserting the needle in the right side of pleat #3 and stitching through pleat. Again, pull the thread downward.

Step 4

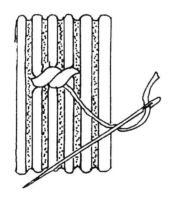

Step 5

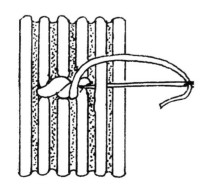

Return the thread to the "above the needle" position and continue across the panel for the required number of stitches.

STEM STITCH

The stem stitch is smocked from left to right and the thread will ALWAYS be held below the needle. Each individual stitch will slant obliquely from the upper left to the lower right making a "Z" curve. Do not slant the needle. The needle will always be held parallel to the gathering threads.

Step 1

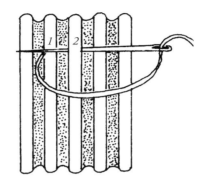

Bring the needle out of the left side of pleat #1 about $^2/_3$ to $^3/_4$ of the pleat depth. Enter the fabric at the right side of pleat #2—stitch through pleat #2.

Step 2

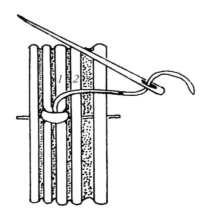

Pull floss upward after the first (and each) stitch.

Step 3

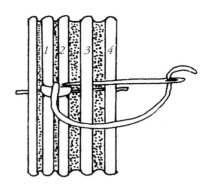

Take the floss to the "below the needle" position. Smock the next stitch by inserting the needle in the right side of pleat #3 and stitching through the pleat. Pull thread upward after each stitch.

Step 4

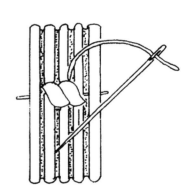

Step 5

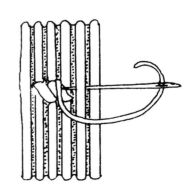

Return floss to the "below the needle" position. Continue across the pleated fabric for the required number of stitches.

WAVE STITCHES

The full-step wave and the half-step or baby wave are the simplest of wave stitches. This stitch is very elastic—the deeper the wave, the more elasticity it will have.

The full-step wave covers the space between two gathering rows. The half-step or baby wave covers one-half the space between two gathering rows. As with previous stitches, the wave is smocked from the left to the right side of the gathered fabric. The needle is always inserted parallel to the gathering threads and perpendicular to the pleats.

Step 1

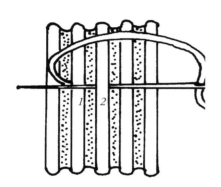

Begin stitching by bringing the needle out of the left side of pleat #1 about $^2/_3$ to $^3/_4$ of the pleat depth. The floss should be above the needle. Bring the needle over pleat #1 and enter the fabric at the right side of pleat #2. Stitch through pleat #2. This stitch will be the "cap" of the wave.

Step 2

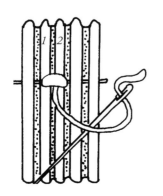

Pull the floss downward after the first stitch and after each upper or "cap" stitch. Do not pull too tightly.

Step 3

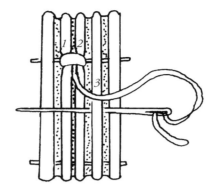

Bring the needle down to the bottom of the wave (usually $^1/_2$ or full space). Move over the pleat #3 and stitch through pleat #3 from right to left side. Be sure the floss is pulled to the side to avoid stitching over it.

Step 4 and 5

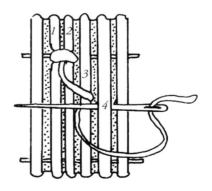

Pull the floss downward to form the "leg," angled from the upper left to the lower right. At the same level, stitch through pleat #4 to form the lower level stitch or "foot" of the wave.

Step 6

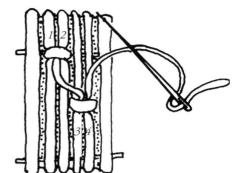

Pull the floss upward to tighten the "foot." Do not pull too tightly.

Step 7

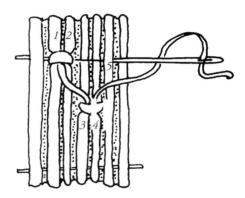

Return to the same level as the first stitch and stitch through pleat #5. Pull gently upward to form the "leg" angled from lower left to upper right.

Be sure that the floss is pulled to the side to avoid stitching over it.

Step 8

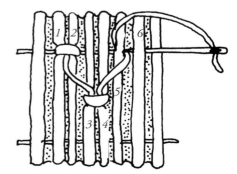

Stitch through pleat #6 to form the upper or "cap" stitch.

Step 9

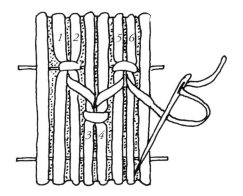

Gently pull floss downward and repeat stitching sequence to complete design.

TRELLIS WAVE

The trellis wave can cover from a half-space to several gathering rows. This stitch is basically the same as the wave stitch except that there may be several stitches on each side of the wave rather than one long stitch.

The trellis wave is smocked from the left side to the right side of the gathered fabric. The needle is always inserted parallel to the gathering threads and perpendicular to the pleats.

Begin stitching by bringing the needle out of the left side of pleat #1 at about $2/3$ to $3/4$ of the pleat depth.

Step 1

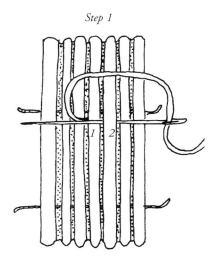

The floss should be above the needle. Bring the needle over pleat #1 and re-enter the fabric on the right side of pleat #2. Stitch through pleat #2. This stitch will be the "cap" of the wave.

Step 2

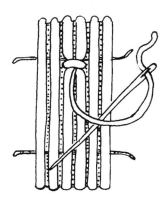

Pull the floss downward after this first stitch and after each upper or "cap" stitch. Do not pull too tightly.

Step 3

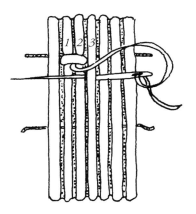

Bring the needle down one step. (Example: For a 3-step wave over one space, visually divide the space between the gathering threads into three equal parts. This first step or stitch will be at the $1/3$ row mark.) Move over to pleat #3 and stitch through pleat #3 from right to left. Be sure that the floss is pulled to the side to avoid stitching over it. Pull the floss gently downward.

Step 4

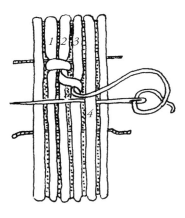

Bring the needle down one step (for a 3-step trellis, this stitch as at the $2/3$ row mark). Move over to pleat #4 and stitch through pleat #4. Pull downward gently.

Bring needle down to the next mark (example is to full row mark). Move over to pleat #5 and stitch through pleat #5 on the row.

Step 5

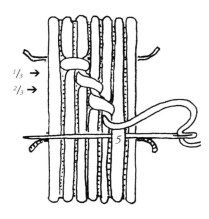

Pull downward gently. This will complete the "leg" which is angled downward from the upper left to the lower right.

At the same level as the previous stitch, stitch through pleat #6 (thread will lay below the needle when making this "foot" stitch).

Step 6

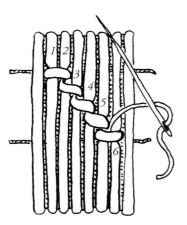

Pull upward gently to form the lower level or "foot" of the trellis wave.

Step 9

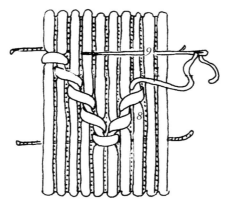

Step 11

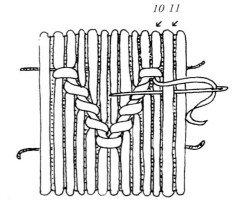

Gently pull floss downward and repeat sequence to complete the trellis wave row.

Step 7

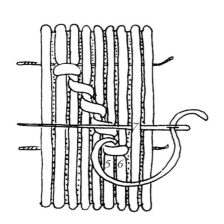

Steps 7-8-9 show stitching of the "leg" which is angled upward. Begin by bringing the needle up to the $^1/_3$ mark and stitch through pleat #7, keeping the thread below the needle. Next, stitch through pleat #8 at $^2/_3$ mark. For the third step of the trellis, stitch through pleat #9 at upper gathering row.

Step 10

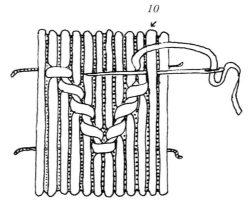

With the thread held above the needle, stitch through pleat #10 on upper gathering row to from the top level stitch or "cap" stitch.

Step 8

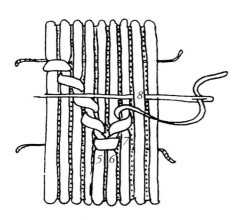

Buttons 'n' Bows
14086 Memorial Drive
Houston TX 77079
Phone: (281) 496-0170; (800) 769-3251

Fine fabrics for heirloom sewing and smocking. Imported laces and embroideries. Smocking plates, patterns, books, doll kits and ready-to-smock garments. Pleating service and classes.

Carol Harris Company
206B East Court Street
Dyersburg TN 38024
Phone: (901) 285-9419
e-mail: carolh@usit.net

We carry the finest fabrics, laces and trims for children's and adult garments. Planning and construction of children's clothing is our specialty. Mail orders welcome.

Roberta Chase
528 Hillside Terrace
West Orange NJ 07052
e-mail: Bibbi123@aol.com

The princess lace tape "Teardrop Jabot" kit is available for $8.50 ppd. (white, black or ecru) as well as a complete line of princess lace materials. Also available are other fine handsewing and embroidery materials. Send a LSASE for a brochure.

Children's Corner
3814 Cleghorn Avenue
Nashville TN 37215
Phone: (800) 543-6915 (orders);
    (615) 292-1746 (retail store)
Fax: (615) 385-0837

Children's Corner carries an excellent variety of heirloom fabrics, laces, trims, buttons, patterns, smocking plates and books. Services include pleating and custom garments. Catalog available for $2.50.

Classic Creations
P.O. Box 4204
Crofton MD 21114
e-mail: Megerstch@aol.com

Send LSASE for brochure. Ready-to-smock ornament kits; source for Needle Necessities floss overdyed, floche, Kreinik metallics and stranded silk, needles, wire edge ribbon, and Sudberry House accessories.

Dancing Needles
2717 Lebanon Road
Nashville TN 37214
Phone: (615) 885-0898

We carry antique, vintage laces, tatting, mother-of-pearl & specialty buttons, silk ribbon, silk floss, floche, Battenburg, princess and lace tapes, fine needlework books, fine fabrics. Our services include pleating, covered buttons, custom orders.

Denham Designs
P.O. Box 241275
Memphis TN 38124-1275
Phone: (800) 451-7143; (901) 683-4574

Mail order only. Heirloom sewing and smocking supplies. Patterns, plates, books, fabric, 57 colors Imperial broadcloth all discounted. Expect expert service and prompt shipments domestic or overseas.

Fashion Fabrics & All Brand Sewing
9789 Florida Blvd.
Baton Rouge LA 70815
Phone: Machines (504) 923-1282;
    (800) 739-7374
Phone: Fabrics (504) 923-1260;
    (800) 627-1260
Fax: (504) 923-1261; (800) 866-1261
e-mail: sewserg@aol.com
Web: www.allbrands.com

Fashion/heirloom fabrics, laces, lace tapes, books, patterns, plates, silk ribbon, silk/cotton/rayon hand & machine embroidery threads, machines, repair, pleating, buttonholes, etc.

Gardner's Ribbons & Lace
2235 E. Division
Arlington TX 76011
Phone: (817) 640-1436
Fax: (817) 640-1436

The finest in ribbons, laces, buttons, beads, trimmings and Swiss fabrics. Extensive color ranges and width selection. Domestic and imports. Heirloom to bridal. Antique. Boutique. Unique. "Ribbon Chocolate" kit available.

Heirlooms Forever
3112 Cliff Gookin Boulevard
Tupelo MS 38801
Phone: (601) 842-4275; (800) 840-4275
Fax: (601) 842-2284
Web: www.sews.com

Heirlooms Forever offers the quilter, smocker or heirloomist the finest variety of supplies through its web site, toll free ordering or superior shop customer service. Please join our family of customers and let us turn your sewing frustrations into Heirlooms Forever.

Kiyo Design, Inc.
11 Annapolis Street
Annapolis MD 21401
Phone: (410) 280-1942
Fax: (410) 280-2793
e-mail: Kiyosew@IBM.net
Web: http://www.kiyoinc.com/fabric.html

Retail store and mail order service offering the finest fabrics, laces, embroideries, ribbons, beads, buttons, threads and notions for smocking, embroidery, heirloom and fine fashion sewing.

Ladida Fine Fabrics, Inc.
4726 Poplar Avenue
Memphis TN 38117
Phone: (901) 761-4316

A full-service shop; mail orders welcome.
We offer a pleating service, and carry
many hard-to-find classic smocking
plates. Ask about our antique laces and
our fabulous button collection.

Linda's Silver Needle
200 East 5th Avenue, Suite 125
P.O. Box 2167
Naperville IL 60567
Phone: (800) SMOCK-IT
Fax: (800) 739-2468
Web: www.silverneedle.com

Let us bring our charming specialty
sewing shop right to your mailbox. Call
about our newsletter filled with
wonderful fabric swatches and all the
latest in specialty sewing supplies.

Miss Maureen's Fabrics and Fancies
5763 Airport Blvd.
Mobile AL 36608
Phone: (334) 343-8270; (800) 699-0991
Fax: (334) 343-8390

Let us inspire, teach, guide and supply
you in every aspect of sewing. Twenty
types of embroidery threads, 14 machine
threads, 17 types of needles, 40 pattern
designers. Thread kit for "Candy Dress"
available. Full line of Viking products.

Olde Sew 'n So
4450 Hugh Howell Road
Shop #8
Tucker GA 30084
Phone: (770) 496-5505

We are an heirloom smocking shop and
authorized Elna dealer. We carry a full
line of laces, fabrics and notions, along
with teaching a wide variety of classes.
Mail orders are welcomed.

Pintucks & Pinafores
4200 Paces Ferry Road
Vinings Jubilee Suite 476
Atlanta GA 30339
Phone: (770) 384-1216; (888) 342-6478
Fax: (770) 384-1218
e-mail: pintucks@bellsouth.net

We offer a wide selection of cotton
prints, silks, linens and laces, DMC
flosses, and YLI silk floss and ribbon.
Extensive line of patterns & smocking
plates. Porcelain and ceramic buttons,
antique buttons, brass and pewter
buttons, and even chenille buttons.

Sew Fancy
RR#1 Beeton
Ontario, Canada L0G 1A0
Phone: 1(905) 775-1396;
1-800-SEW-FNCY
Fax: 1(905) 775-0107
e-mail: sewfancy@interhop.net
Web: www.sewfancy.com

Canada's larges source for heirloom
sewing, smocking, embroidery, lingerie
and bra making supplies. Catalog $5.
Retail store open 10-4 Monday-Saturday.
Foreign orders welcome.

Sewing Treasures
2718 Devine Street
Columbia SC 29205
Phone: (803) 252-8585
Fax: (803) 252-8552

We offer a complete line of smocking and
heirloom sewing supplies—fabrics, laces,
patterns, floche, silk floss, books, notions,
classes, pleating, construction. Mail order
welcome.

Sew So Fancy
914 Queen City Avenue
Tuscaloosa AL 35401
Phone: (205) 759-4691; (800) 821-0607

A specialty shop offering the finest in
imported lace, fabrics, books and notions
for creating heirloom clothing. Beautiful
baby gifts, nursery accessories and gifts.
Classic ready-mades for children.

Sew Unique
626 15th Street E
Tuscaloosa AL 35401
Phone: (800) 837-8799
Fax: (205) 752-9300

We have everything you need to create
special frocks. Custom orders are also
available.

Smock and Sew
2211 21st Avenue South
Nashville TN 37212-4907
Phone: (615) 269-5177

Just a call away—mail order source for
large selection of fabrics, heirloom and
smocking supplies, batistes, laces, eyelets,
specialty threads, buttons, patterns and
books.

Smocked Togs Inc.
Virginia Fletcher Lane
812 South Cottage Avenue
Independence MO 64050
Phone: (816) 254-5204

Smocked Togs offers smocking supplies,
pleating service, French laces, Swiss
batiste, Imperial broadcloth, batiste,
tartans & micro-checks, custom-made
children's clothing. Call for mail order
and our retail catalog.

The Heirloom Iron Bed Company
10800 Alpharetta Hwy. #188
Roswell GA 30076
Phone: (770)993-7249
Fax: (770)993-9703

One look at our collection of magnificent
brass beds will tell you why the South is
in no hurry to awaken! Our beds come
with an ironclad guarantee—they'll be
here for you, for your children, and your
children's children.

The Pin Cushion
2307 North Alexander Drive
Baytown TX 77520
Phone: (281) 427-6414
Fax: (281) 428-1030

We carry Husqvarna/Viking sewing
machines and sergers,
digitizing/customizing software and
training, and a complete line of HORN
Sewing furniture. Complete notions and
library sections support our fine selection
of fabrics, including quilting fabric.

The Sewing Studio, Inc.
1310 S. Memorial Blvd.
Martinsville VA 24112
Phone: (800)220-2249; (540) 632-5700
Fax: (540) 632-5700 (dual phone & fax
line)
e-mail: jfeeny@neocomm.net

Located in the foothills of Virginia, we
sell Elna and BabyLock machines.
Predominately a quilt shop, we carry
hard-to-find specialty threads, heirloom
and needlework supplies.

The Smocking Bird
2917 Linden Avenue
Birmingham AL 35209
Phone: (205) 879-SMOC (7662)

The largest antique lace and heirloom
fabric selection in the South! Pima prints,
stripes, checks and solids—lots of Liberty.
Great selection of patterns and plates.
Mail orders welcome.

The Smocking Bonnet
16012 Frederick Road (Rt. 144)
P.O. Box 53
Lisbon MD 21765-0053
Phone: (800) 524-1678; (410) 489-7110
Web:
http://www.quikpage.com/s/smocking

Friendly service; same day response on
most orders. Pleating service, lessons and
free advice. Retail hours 10-4 weekdays;
10-2 Saturdays. Closed holidays.

The Smocking Horse Collection
5 Parkway Drive
Olmstead Falls OH 44138
Phone: (440) 235-2035; (800) 910-2035
Fax: 440-235-0578

Recapture the joy of sewing with our
heirloom fabrics and laces, children and
adult fabrics, sewing supplies and Janice
Andrews Balliett's smocking designs.
Catalog—$5.

Threads of Time
10225 Main St.
Clarence NY 14031-2013
Phone/Fax: (716) 759-0710

Smocking and heirloom shop filled with
fine fabrics, imported laces, variety of
Battenburg tapes, books and patterns.
Custom pleating service. PFAFF Sewing
Machine Sales & Service.

Tosca Company
13503 Tosca Lane, Suite 200
Houston TX 77079
Phone: (713) 984-8545
(800) 290-8327

We offer pleaters for English smocking,
the Sally Stanley 24-row, the Pullen 16-
row and the Amanda Jane 16- and 24-
row machines.